Teacher's Book

A RESOURCE FOR PLANNING AND TEACHING

Level K WOW! Wonder of Words

Senior Authors J. David Cooper, John J. Pikulski

Authors Kathryn H. Au, Margarita Calderón, Jacqueline C. Comas, Marjorie Y. Lipson, J. Sabrina Mims, Susan E. Page, Sheila W. Valencia, MaryEllen Vogt

Consultants Dolores Malcolm, Tina Saldivar, Shane Templeton

INVITATIONS TO LITERACY

Houghton Mifflin Company • Boston

Atlanta • Dallas • Geneva, Illinois • Palo Alto • Princeton

Acknowledgments

Grateful acknowledgment is made for permission to reprint copyrighted material as follows:

A Birthday Basket For Tia, by Pat Mora, illustrated by Cecily Lang. Text copyright © 1992 by Pat Mora. Illustrations copyright © 1992 by Cecily Lang. Reprinted by permission of Macmillan Books for Young Readers, Simon & Schuster Children's Publishing Division.

Animal Mothers, by Atsushi Komori, illustrated by Masayuki Yabuuchi. Text copyright © 1983 by Atsushi Komori. Illustrations copyright © 1983 Masayuki Yabuuchi. Reprinted by permission of The Putnam & Grosset Group.

"I Saw a Purple Cow," from *I Saw a Purple Cow and 100 Other Recipes for Learning,* by Ann S. Cole et al. Copyright © 1972 by Ann S. Cole, Carolyn B. Haas, Faith P. Bushnell, and Betty K. Weinberger. Reprinted by permission of Little, Brown and Company and Curtis Brown Ltd.

Me Too! written and illustrated by Mercer Mayer. Copyright © 1983 by Mercer Mayer. Reprinted by permission of Western Publishing Company, Inc.

Mr. Gumpy's Outing, written and illustrated by John Burningham. Copyright © 1970 by John Burningham. Reprinted by permission of Henry Holt & Company, Inc.

My Big Dictionary, by the Editors of the American Heritage Dictionaries, illustrated by Pamela Cote. Copyright © 1994 by Houghton Mifflin Company. All rights reserved.

"My Family," from *Rhymes About Us,* by Marchette Chute. Copyright © 1974 by Marchette Chute. Reprinted by permission of Elizabeth Roach.

"Others Are Special," by Lois Raebeck, from *Who Am I?*. Copyright © 1970 by Lois Raebeck. Reprinted by permission of the author.

"Our Family," by Linda Arnold. Copyright © 1988 by Linda Arnold Publishing. Reprinted by permission of Linda Arnold Publishing.

Ten Black Dots, by Donald Crews. Copyright © 1968, 1986 by Donald Crews. Reprinted by permission of Greenwillow Books, a division of William Morrow & Company, Inc.

Ten In A Bed, by Mary Rees. Copyright © 1988 by Mary Rees. Reprinted by permission of Little, Brown and Company.

"Travel Plans," from *Upside Down and Inside Out,* by Bobbi Katz. Copyright © 1973 by Bobbi Katz. Reprinted by permission of the author.

"Yesterday's Paper," by Mabel Watts. Protected by copyright. All rights reserved.

Photography Credits

THEME: Just for Fun

Cathy Copeland, pp. T27, T31, T32, T62, T63, T88, T91; John Lei, pp. T61, T84; Tony Scarpetta, pp. T58; Tracey Wheeler, pp. T13, T27, T28, T29, T31, T32, T33, T57, T59, T61, T62, T63, T83, T85, T89, T91, T94
Banta Digital Group, pp. T17, T29, T30, T61, T81, T89; Donald Crews, p.T34; Tara Hinemann, p.T14

THEME: Family Time

Cathy Copeland, pp. T118, T119, T124, T153; John Lei, pp. T121, T145, T151, T175, T176, T184, T186; Tracey Wheeler, pp. T105, T121, T123, T125, T145, T147, T149, T151, T153, T173, T175, T177, T181, T183
Banta Digital Group, pp. T119, T123, T143, T145, T146, T147, T148, T152, T172, T173, T174, T176, T177, T181, T182; Kindra Clineff p.154; Steve Ogilvy, p.T122

Printed in U.S.A.

ISBN: 0-395-79543-5
23456789-B-99 98 97

Just for Fun

Table of Contents
THEME: Just for Fun

Big Book *LITERATURE FOR WHOLE CLASS AND SMALL GROUP INSTRUCTION*

by **Mary Rees**

fiction

Ten in a Bed

An amusing version of the traditional song.

WATCH ME READ Books *PRACTICE FOR ORAL LANGUAGE AND STORYTELLING*

Surprise!

Illustrated by Susan Meddaugh

Each title is also available in black and white. This version includes a home activity.

Bibliography

Books for the Library Corner

 Multicultural

 Science/Health

 Math

 Social Studies

 Music

 Art

The Alphabet in Nature
by Judy Feldman
Childrens 1991 (32p)
Close observation reveals the letters of the alphabet in photographs of nature. (wordless)

Hiccup
by Mercer Mayer
Dial 1976 (32p) Puffin 1993 paper
In a funny adventure, an elephant helps his friend Ms. Hippo get rid of the hiccups. (wordless)

Jiggle Wiggle Prance
by Sally Noll
Puffin 1993 (32p)
Lively animals act out action words like *climb, ride,* and *jump.*

Alphabatics
by Suse MacDonald
Macmillan 1986
(64p) also paper
Letters of the alphabet transform into pictures that illustrate the letter's sound. (wordless)

The Lifesize Animal Counting Book
 Dorling Kindersley 1994 (32p)
Big-as-life photos of animals like rabbits and tortoises make counting fun.

Animal Antics
 Snap Shot 1994 (32p)
Photographs introduce readers to animals like playful seals and chatty chimps.

The Cat Sat on the Mat
by Alice Cameron
Houghton 1994 (32p)
As children look through a peep-hole to guess where the family cat is going next, they learn new words.

Houses Around Our World
 by The National Geographic Society
National Geographic 1994 (18p)
Readers are brought inside the homes of families from other cultures.

Elephants Aloft
by Kathi Appelt
Harcourt 1993 (32p)
Two elephants fly above rooftops, below the moon, and across oceans as they travel by balloon to Africa.

Funny Faces
 Snapshot 1994 (32p)
Photographs focus on animal faces that are both strange and familiar.

Books for Teacher Read Aloud

What's for Lunch?
by John Schindel
Lothrop 1994 (32p)
A cumulative series of animals almost interrupt Sydney the mouse's plans for a picnic lunch.

Dogs Don't Wear Sneakers
by Laura Joffe Numeroff
Simon 1993 (32p)
A child imagines animals doing all kinds of wacky things.

Shape Space
⭐ *by Catherine Falwell*
Clarion 1992 (32p)
A young girl dances her way through geometric shapes.

Don't Forget the Bacon!
by Pat Hutchins
Greenwillow 1976 (32p) Mulberry 1989 paper
A trip to the store turns into a funny excursion when a boy mixes up the grocery list.

The Absent-Minded Toad
by Javier Rondón
Kane/Miller 1994 (32p)
During a shopping expedition a toad has such fun that he forgets to buy anything. **Available in Spanish as El sapo distraído.**

Blackberry Ink
by Eve Merriam
Morrow 1985 (32p) Mulberry 1994 paper
Pizza, cats, and a washing machine are some of the subjects of this collection of bouncy poems.

Guess Who?
⭐ *by Margaret Miller*
Greenwillow 1994 (40p)
Simple questions and a series of possible answers engage children in a guessing game.

Max Found Two Sticks
⭐ *by Brian Pinkney*
Simon 1994 (32p)
Max uses sticks to tap out the rhythms of the things he sees and hears around him.

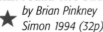

The Quiet Noisy Book
by Margaret Wise Brown
Harper 1950 (32p)
The little dog Muffin tries to figure out what quiet sound woke him from his sleep.

Caps for Sale
by Esphyr Slobodkina
Harper 1947 (48p) also paper
A band of mischievous monkeys makes off with a peddler's hats.
Available in Spanish as Se venden gorras.

You Can't Catch Me!
⭐ *by Annabel Collis*
Little 1993 (32p)
A little boy's imagination transforms a city playground into a jungle.

Minerva Louise
by Janet Morgan Stoeke
Dutton 1988 (32p) Puffin paper
A hen named Minerva Louise explores a house searching for a playmate.

The Sheep Follow
by Monica Wellington
Dutton 1992 (32p)
After following different animals, sheep are too tired to follow their shepherd.

Aaron and Gayla's Counting Book
⭐ *by Eloise Greenfield*
Black Butterfly 1994 (32p)
Two children playing in the rain count the things around them.

Books for Shared Reading

Today Is Monday

by Eric Carle
Philomel 1993 (32p)
A favorite song introduces readers to the days of the week.

Five Little Monkeys Jumping on the Bed
by Eileen Christelow
Clarion 1989 (32p) also paper
Trouble starts when five little monkeys jump on the bed after they say goodnight to their mama.

Los pollitos dicen/The Baby Chicks Sing: Traditional Games, Nursery Rhymes, and Songs from Spanish-Speaking Countries

by Nancy Abraham Hall and Jill Syverson-Stork
Little 1994
This collection of songs and rhymes celebrates playtime.
In English and Spanish.

Thump, Thump, Rat-a-Tat-Tat

by Gene Baer
Harper 1989 (32p)
A marching band grows louder and louder as it approaches.

Sheep on a Ship
by Nancy Shaw
Houghton 1989 (32p)
A group of zany sheep share funny adventures on a pirate ship.

The House That Jack Built

by Jenny Stow
Dial 1992 (32p)
A Caribbean setting gives a favorite nursery rhyme lush new life.

Peanut Butter and Jelly: A Play Rhyme
by Nadine Bernard Westcott
Puffin 1992 (24p)
With the help of elephants and a baker, two children make an enormous sandwich.

Each Peach Pear Plum
by Janet and Allan Ahlberg
Viking 1978 (32p) Puffin paper
In a rhyming game of I Spy, children find familiar nursery rhyme characters.

Ten Pink Piglets: Garth Pig's Wall Song
by Mary Rayner
Dutton 1994 (32p)
This song counts down from one to ten as successive piglets tumble off a wall.

Technology Resources

Computer Software

Internet See the Houghton Mifflin **Internet** resources for additional bibliographic entries and theme-related activities.

Video Cassettes

Alphabatics *by Suse MacDonald.* SRA Media

Pigs *by Robert Munsch.* Media Basics

Curious George *by H. A. Rey.* Media Basics

Audio Cassettes

Ride a Purple Pelican *by Jack Prelutsky.* Listening Library

As I Was Crossing Boston Common *by Norma Farber.* Listening Library

Caps for Sale *by Esphyr Slobodkina.* Weston Woods

Mr. Gumpy's Motor Car *by John Burningham.* Weston Woods

Filmstrips

Brian Wildsmith's Circus *by Brian Wildsmith.* Weston Woods

Bubble Bubble *by Mercer Mayer.* Weston Woods

Each Peach Pear Plum *by Janet and Allan Ahlberg.* Weston Woods

Mr. Gumpy's Outing *by John Burningham.* Weston Woods

AV Addresses are in the Teacher's Handbook, pp. H15-H16.

Theme at a Glance

Reading/Listening Center

Selections	Comprehension Skills and Strategies	Phonemic Awareness	Concept Development	Concepts About Print	
Mr. Gumpy's Outing	✔ Noting details, T23, T28 A new idea for Mr. Gumpy, T28 Warning signs, T28 Reading strategies, T18, T20, T24 **Rereading/responding,** T26-T27	✔ Producing rhyming words, T25, T29 Animals and the things they do, T29 Animal guessing game, T29	Questions and answers, T19 Animal names and sounds, T21		
Ten Black Dots	✔ Sequence, T43, T56 What number will come next?, T56 Placing numbers in order, T56 Reading strategies, T38, T40, T46, T50, T52 **Rereading/responding,** T54-T55		Numeral identification, T41 Number/object equivalents (1-10), T47 Adding 1 to the numbers 1-9, T53 Reviewing *Aa* through *Mm*, T57 Favorite colors, T57 Numerals and numbers, T57 Number match, T57	✔ Spoken word as word, T45, T58 Return sweep, T51 Concentration, T58 Creating new verses, T58	
Ten in a Bed	✔ Cause and effect, T69, T82 A new ending, T82 Guessing sounds, T82 Reading strategies, T68, T70, T72, T76, T78 **Rereading/responding,** T80-T81		Feelings, T71 Number words 1-10, T73 Numbers: subtracting, T79, T83 Number countdown, T83 Letter name review, T83	✔ Written word as word, T75, T84 Pillow toss, T84	

✔ *Indicates Tested Skills. See page T11 for assessment options.*

Theme Concept

There are many different kinds of humor.

Pacing

This theme is designed to take $2\frac{1}{2}$ to 3 weeks, depending on your students' needs.

Multi-Age Classroom

This theme can be used in conjunction with themes found in another grade level.
Grade 1: Get the Giggles

Language/Writing Center

Cross-Curricular Center

Listening	Oral Language	Writing	Content Areas
	Sharing outings, T30 Action words, T30 Traveling words, T30 Identifying action words, T30	Tea party menu, T31 A favorite outing, T31 A silly animal, T31	**Music:** creating a new verse, T32 **Art:** making styrofoam boats, T32 **Math:** passenger count, T33 **Social Studies:** discussing workers on a ship, T33
Rhyming words, T59 Word toss, T59 Playing giant steps, T59	Saving money, T60 Identifying numbers, T60 Word clues, T60	Class counting book, T37 Ideas using colored dots, T61 Writing about an illustration, T61 Animals with spots, T61	**Math:** identifying number shapes, T62 **Music:** musical numbers, T62 **Science:** examining water dots, T63 **Art:** creative creations, T63
Listen for directions, T85 Rhyming words, T85 Playing telephone, T85	Word web, T88 The personality of the little one, T88 Tear-and-take story, T88	A sleepover, T67 Message board, T87 Ways to have fun, T87 Something silly, T89 Adapting a story, T89 Times of day, T89	**Health:** a good night's sleep, T90 **Math:** naming numbers, T90 **Art:** make a bed, T91 **Drama:** acting out the ending, T91

Meeting Individual Needs

Key to Meeting Individual Needs

Students Acquiring English

Activities and notes throughout the lesson plans offer strategies to help children understand the selections and lessons.

Challenge

Challenge activities and notes throughout the lesson plans suggest additional activities to stimulate critical and creative thinking.

Extra Support

Activities and notes throughout the lesson plans offer additional strategies to help children experience success.

Managing Instruction

Following Directions

No matter how simple you make instructions, young children will ask you to repeat them. Begin by introducing a few consistent procedures that children can learn to do automatically. As each new procedure is introduced, reinforce the directions by drawing the steps on a chart or chalkboard; making it into a chant, rhyme, or song; or having students model for each other. Walk children through each step as a whole class. As you do, work on active listening skills such as making eye contact and noting direction words.

For further information on this and other Managing Instruction topics, see the *Professional Development Handbook*.

Performance Standards

During this theme, children will

- *recognize ways that stories are fun and interesting*
- *make predictions and inferences about story characters and events*
- *retell or summarize each selection*
- *apply comprehension skills: Noting Details, Sequence, Cause and Effect*
- *recognize spoken words as words*
- *produce rhymes in speech*
- *write a story*

Students Acquiring English	Challenge	Extra Support
Develop Key Concepts Children focus on Key Concepts through dramatization and playing rhyming, guessing, number, and word games.	**Apply Critical Thinking** Children apply critical thinking by noting details, learning number sequence, discussing cause and effect, and exploring number equivalents.	**Receive Increased Instructional Time** Practice activities in the Reading/Listening Center provide support with noting details, sequence, and cause and effect. Children also work on producing rhyming words.
Act as a Resource Children are asked to share animal sounds in their native language.	**Explore Topics of Interest** Activities that motivate further exploration include exploring places children would like to visit and experimenting with floating and sinking.	**Provide Independent Reading** Children choose to explore books and to read independently when exciting, theme-related literature is made available (see Bibliography, T6-T7).
Expand Vocabulary Throughout the theme, children use context and picture clues, discuss meanings, and model definitions. Children expand their vocabulary to include action words and numerals.	**Engage in Creative Thinking** Opportunities for creative expression include acting out emotions, making a book, and writing invitations.	

Additional Resources

Invitaciones

Develop bi-literacy with this integrated reading/language arts program in Spanish. Provides authentic literature and real-world resources from Spanish-speaking cultures.

Language Support

Translations of Big Books in Chinese, Hmong, Khmer, and Vietnamese. *Teacher's Booklet* provides instructional support in English.

Students Acquiring English Handbook

Guidelines, strategies, and additional instruction for students acquiring English.

Planning for Assessment

Informal Assessment

Observation Checklists

- Concepts About Print/Book Handling
- Responding to Literature and Decoding Behaviors and Strategies
- Writing Behaviors and Stages of Temporary Spelling
- Listening and Speaking Behaviors
- Story Retelling and Rereading

Literacy Activity Book

- Produces Rhymes, p. 31
- Personal Response, p. 32
- Comprehension: Sequence, p. 34
- Language Patterns, p. 38
- Subtracting Numbers, p. 41

Retellings—Oral/Written

- *Teacher's Assessment Handbook*

Formal Assessment

Kindergarten Literacy Survey

Evaluates children's literacy development. Provides holistic indicator of children's ability with:

- Shared Reading/ Constructing Meaning
- Concepts About Print
- Phonemic Awareness
- Emergent Writing

Theme Skills Test

- Sequence
- Rhymes

Portfolio Assessment

The portfolio icon signals portfolio opportunities throughout the theme.

Additional Portfolio Tips:

- Evaluating *Literacy Activity Book* Pages, T93

Launching the Theme

See the Houghton Mifflin **Internet** resources for theme-related activities.

Song Tape for Just For Fun: *"John Jacob Jingleheimer Schmidt"*

INTERACTIVE LEARNING

Warm-up

Singing the Theme Song

Invite children to sing a silly song about a man with a funny name. Play the song "John Jacob Jingleheimer Schmidt" on the Song Tape. (For lyrics see the Teacher's Handbook, H10)

After singing the song once, brainstorm with children some other silly names to replace John Jacob Jingleheimer Schmidt and write their suggestions on the board. Then have children make up new verses, using some of these silly names.

Interactive Bulletin Board

Fun Is Everywhere Children will enjoy adding to and talking about the fun pictures in the balloons on the bulletin board. Throughout the theme, alternate the pictures inside the balloons. Some ideas:

- Have children cut pictures of people and animals having fun or being silly from magazines and paste them on the balloons.

- Invite children to draw and paste a picture of themselves in their favorite fun place on the balloons.

- Some children may want to bring in photos of themselves having fun and paste them inside balloons.

See the *Home/Community Connections Booklet* for theme-related materials.

Ongoing Project

Fun Box

Designate a large decorated box as the Fun Box. Some ideas of things to put in the box and activities to do with them include:

- Put old hats, scarves, ties, and other "dress up" clothes in the box for role-playing.

- Invite children to make masks of animal characters to keep in the box for story retellings and dramatizations.

- At the conclusion of the theme, children can gather materials from the Fun Box for a costume party and theme celebration.

Portfolio Opportunity

The Portfolio Opportunity icon highlights portfolio opportunities throughout the theme.

Choices for Centers

Creating Centers

Use these activities to create learning centers in the classroom.

Reading/Listening Center

- Warning: Beware!, T28
- Order the Numbers, T56
- Pillow Toss, T84

Language/Writing Center

- A Favorite Outing, T 31
- A Dot of a Different Color T 61
- I'm in the Bed, T89

Cross-Curricular Center

- Math: Passenger Count, T33
- Science: Water Dots, T63
- Art: Make a Bed, T 91

READ ALOUD

SELECTION:

Mr. Gumpy's Outing

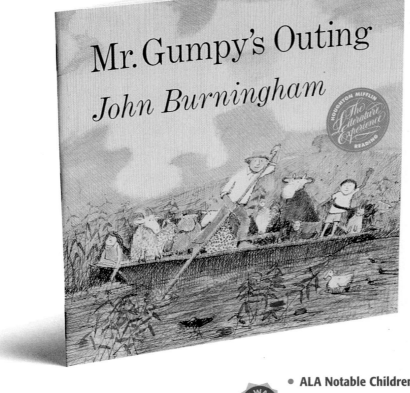

by John Burningham

Other Books by the Author

Avocado Baby

Granpa

John Patrick Norman McHennessey:The Boy Who Was Always Late

- ALA Notable Children's Book
- Boston Globe-Horn Book Honor Book
- Kate Greenaway Medal
- New York Times Best Illustrated Children's Book of the Year
- Best Books for Children
- Library of Congress Children's Book of the Year
- SLJ Best Book
- Children's Book Showcase

Selection Summary

In this cumulative story, Mr. Gumpy sets out on a boat ride. When two children ask for a ride, Mr. Gumpy agrees but warns them not to squabble. Along the way, several animals ask for a ride. Mr. Gumpy lets them all on the boat but warns them about the things they shouldn't do. In spite of his cautions, inevitably the children and the animals all begin to move and make noise, which causes the boat to tip. In the end, they dry off and make it home in time for tea.

Lesson Planning Guide

	Skill/Strategy Instruction	Meeting Individual Needs	Lesson Resources
1 **Introduce** *the* **Literature** *Pacing: 1 day*	**Preparing to Listen and Write** Warm-up/Build Background, T16 Read Aloud, T16	Choices for Rereading, T17 **Students Acquiring English, T17**	**Poster** Row, Row, Row Your Boat, T16 *Literacy Activity Book* Personal Response, p. 29 **Story Props,** T17
2 **Interact** *with* **Literature** *Pacing: 1–2 days*	**Reading Strategies** Predict/Infer, T18, T24 Summarize, T20 **Minilessons** Questions and Answers, T19 Animal Names and Sounds, T21 ✓ Noting Details, T23 ✓ Producing Rhyming Words, T25	**Students Acquiring English,** T21, T26, T27 **Extra Support,** T19, T23 **Rereading and Responding,** T26–T27	**Letter, Word, and Picture Cards,** T21 **Story Props,** T27 See the Houghton Mifflin **Internet** resources for additional activities.
3 **Instruct** *and* **Integrate** *Pacing: 1–2 days*	**Reading/Listening Center** Comprehension, T28 Phonemic Awareness, T29 **Language/Writing Center** Oral Language, T30 Writing, T31 **Cross-Curricular Center** Cross-Curricular Activities, T32–T33	**Students Acquiring English,** T29, T30 **Challenge,** T31, T32, T33 **Extra Support,** T28, T29	**Story Props,** T28 *Literacy Activity Book* Comprehension, p. 30 Phonemic Awareness, p. 31 See the Houghton Mifflin **Internet** resources for additional activities.

✓ *Indicates Tested Skills. See page T11 for assessment options.*

1

Introduce the Literature

Preparing to Listen and Write

Poster

Row, Row, Row Your Boat

Row, row,
row your boat
Gently down
the stream;
Merrily,
merrily,
merrily,
merrily,
Life is
but a dream.

Literacy Activity Book, p. 29

INTERACTIVE LEARNING

Warm-up/Build Background

Sharing a Song

- Ask children to listen and follow along with the song "Row, Row, Row Your Boat" on the poster. As you play the song, children who are familiar with it may want to join in. Then play the song again, encouraging children to pantomime the rowing as they sing along.

- Discuss with children that the person in the song is having a lot of fun rowing the boat "merrily down the stream." Invite children to share any fun experiences they may have had on a boat.

- Point out that in the song, the boat is a row boat and a person rows to make it go. Have children tell about other kinds of boats and what you do to make them go.

- Display the cover of *Mr. Gumpy's Outing.* Point out Mr. Gumpy in the illustration. Ask children what kind of boat Mr. Gumpy has and how he makes it go. Invite children to comment on all the people and animals in Mr. Gumpy's boat.

Reading Aloud
LAB, p. 29

Preview and Predict

Use the cover to point to and read the title and author/illustrator. Have children volunteer to name the animal characters in the boat. Discuss with children what all of these characters might be doing together on a boat and where they might be going. Have them predict what the story is about. Then ask children to listen to find out what happens on Mr. Gumpy's outing.

Read

As you read, pause occasionally to allow children to respond to the story and the illustrations and to predict what might happen after each of the story characters gets on the boat.

Personal Response

Home Connection Have children complete *Literacy Activity Book* page 29. Encourage them to take the page home to share with their families.

Choices for Rereading Aloud

Making Predictions

Reread the story and have children think about what happens in the end. Encourage them to predict what would happen next if the story went on for a few more pages. Ask:

- Do you think the animals will return for another boat ride?
- Do you think the animals will behave?
- Do you think the boat will tip?
- What else might happen?

Rereading with Props

Materials
- Story Retelling Props boat and figures (See Teacher's Handbook, page H2.)

Invite volunteers to use the story prop boat and figures to show what is happening in the story as you reread it. Encourage the class to keep track of how many children and animals get on Mr. Gumpy's boat and in what order.

Students Acquiring English Retelling with props is helpful for children acquiring English. It makes the oral language more comprehensible.

Exploring Language Patterns

Identify the repeated phrase in the text, *Yes, but don't . . .* for children. Then, reread the story and ask them to count the number of times they hear the repeating phrase.

More Choices for Rereading Aloud

In addition to the rereading choices suggested here, you may want to use one or more of the activities suggested on page T26.

- Rereading with Sound and Movement
- Choosing a Funny Scene
- Act It Out

2

Interact
with
Literature

READ ALOUD

Reading Strategies

▶ **Predict/Infer**

Teacher Modeling Remind children that good readers often think about what might happen before they read a story. They also pause during their reading to check whether their ideas are correct. Open to pages 4–5 as you model thinking about the story for children.

Think Aloud

I can tell from the picture of Mr. Gumpy that when he starts on his outing, he is alone in his boat. I know from reading the story already what happens to change his quiet outing, but I wonder what Mr. Gumpy thinks about how the outing turns out.

Purpose Setting

Suggest that as you reread the story, children think (make inferences) about how Mr. Gumpy feels about having company with him on his boat ride

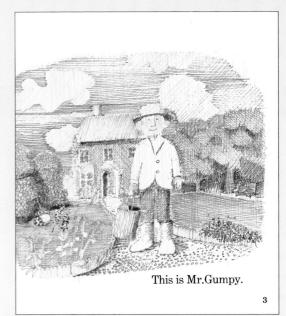

This is Mr. Gumpy.

3

Mr. Gumpy owned a boat and his house was by a river.

4

5

One day Mr. Gumpy went out in his boat.

"May we come with you?" said the children.

"Yes," said Mr. Gumpy,
"if you don't squabble."

6

7

"Can I come along, Mr. Gumpy?"
said the rabbit.

"Yes, but don't hop about."

8

9

MINILESSON

Concept Development
Questions and Answers

Teach/Model

Reread page 6 emphasizing the question in the second line. Point out that the children are asking Mr. Gumpy a question. Read the question again and have them notice that when you read a question, your voice changes a little.

Then point out that Mr. Gumpy answers *"Yes."* Ask children if Mr. Gumpy didn't want the children to ride on the boat, what his answer might be instead. *(No.)*

Practice/Apply

- Reread page 8 and have children identify the question and answer on this page.

- Have children work with a partner to ask and answer a question. One can take the role of Mr. Gumpy and the other can be one of the children or an animal asking to go on Mr. Gumpy's boat.

QuickREFERENCE

Vocabulary

Use the story props of the two children. Create a dialogue between them in which they "squabble" over who gets in the boat first. Ask children if they have ever *squabbled* with someone.

 Extra Support

Some children may understand the idea of Mr. Gumpy going out for the afternoon but not connect this to the word *outing* in the title. Have children share some different kinds of outings they have had.

 Journal

Ask children if they would like to go on Mr. Gumpy's boat. Invite children to draw a picture of themselves on the boat. Have them write or dictate why they think it would be fun to go.

Interact *with* Literature

Reading Strategies

▶ **Summarize**

Tell children that good readers pause sometimes to think about the most important things that have happened so far in a story. Remembering what happens helps them to understand and remember it. Ask children to stop and tell what has happened so far in *Mr. Gumpy's Outing.* *(Mr. Gumpy went for a ride in his boat. Two children asked for a ride and he let them on. Then a rabbit, a cat, and a dog all asked for a ride and Mr. Gumpy let them on the boat too.)*

READ ALOUD

"I'd like a ride," said the cat.

"Very well," said Mr. Gumpy. "But you're not to chase the rabbit."

10

11

"Will you take me with you?" said the dog.

"Yes," said Mr. Gumpy. "But don't tease the cat."

12

13

Quick REFERENCE

Vocabulary

Ask children if anyone has ever *teased* them or if they have ever *teased* someone else. Invite them to offer their own examples. Then ask how the dog might *tease* the cat.

Visual Literacy

Ask children how the picture clues have helped them as you read the story. Have them think about questions such as:
- Is the boat getting too crowded?
- Does Mr. Gumpy look happy or upset?

"May I come, please, Mr. Gumpy?" said the pig.
"Very well, but don't muck about."

14

15

"Have you a place for me?" said the sheep.
"Yes, but don't keep bleating."

16

17

Concept Development
Animal Names and Sounds

Teach/Model

Discuss with children the word *bleat* on page 16. Explain that it tells about the sound a sheep makes. *(baa baa)* Talk about the other animals in the story and the sounds they make.

Materials
● Picture Cards

Practice/Apply

● Have children name animals and tell about or produce the sounds these animals make. Write their ideas on a chart using picture cards and blank strips to write the words.

● Show children an example of a cow with a speech balloon containing "moo." Have children make their own drawings of an animal with a speech balloon containing the sound the animal makes.

Students Acquiring English

Children with different primary languages can tell what animal sounds are in their first language. Discuss how these sounds compare to English animal sounds.

Review

Parts of the Body Use the illustration on page 14 to have children name the parts of the body. You might also compare similarities/differences between animal and human parts of the body. (two legs/four legs, no tail/tail . . .)

Interact *with* Literature

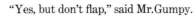

READ ALOUD

"Can we come too?" said the chickens.

"Yes, but don't flap," said Mr. Gumpy.

18

19

"Can you make room for me?" said the calf.

"Yes, if you don't trample about."

20

21

QuickREFERENCE

Vocabulary

Demonstrate or ask children to demonstrate *trample* and explain it means to "stamp or walk heavily."

"May I join you, Mr. Gumpy?" said the goat.

"Very well, but don't kick."

22

23

For a little while they all went along happily
but then...
The goat kicked
The calf trampled
The chickens flapped
The sheep bleated
The pig mucked about
The dog teased the cat
The cat chased the rabbit
The rabbit hopped
The children squabbled
The boat tipped ...

24

25

Math Link

Have children use the illustration on page 22 to count with you the number of people and animals in Mr. Gumpy's boat. (11)

 Extra Support

Reread page 24 with children pantomiming the action of the various animals. Help them to realize the reverse sequence of the children and the animals getting on the boat and the boat eventually tipping.

Review

Recognizes Rhymes Point out that one of the animals' names rhymes with *boat.* Reread the animal names on page 24 and see if children can identify *goat.*

Comprehension

Noting Details

Teach/Model

Point out to children that they may have noticed that Mr. Gumpy and the animals say certain things over and over again. Explain that thinking about what they say will help them figure out what might happen next in the story.

Think Aloud

I know that each time an animal asks Mr. Gumpy for a ride, he always says "Yes." He also tells the animal something it shouldn't do. Sometimes it is the sound the animal makes or the way it moves or acts, but it is always something that the animal likes to do. I know that it's hard to stop doing something you like to do.

Practice/Apply

- Reread pages 18, 20, and 22. Ask children to name each animal and the things Mr. Gumpy says they can't do:

p. 18	chicken → flap
p. 20	calf → trample
p. 22	goat → kick

- Have children use details from page 22 to explain what happens with so many animals in the boat when they start to move around.

SKILL FINDER

Noting Details p. T28

Minilessons,
See Themes 1; 6; 7

Interact *with* Literature

and into the water they fell.

Reading Strategies

▶ Predict/Infer

Have children recall that before reading they thought about how Mr. Gumpy would feel about all the animals joining him on his outing. Include children's reactions with the following questions in a discussion:

- How did you know that Mr. Gumpy liked having the animals as friends? (He let them all join him on the boat, invited them back for tea, and said to come again another day.)

- What might happen if they come for another ride on the boat?

- Would Mr. Gumpy get upset if they tipped the boat again? (Children should infer that since he didn't the first time, he probably would not get upset if it happened again.)

Then Mr. Gumpy and the goat and the calf and the chickens and the sheep and the pig and the dog and the cat and the rabbit and the children all swam to the bank and climbed out to dry in the hot sun.

"We'll walk home across the fields," said Mr. Gumpy. "It's time for tea."

28

29

Self-Assessment

Ask children whether they were confused about anything in the story? What did they do? Help them to ask themselves questions such as:

- Did I look at the pictures?
- Did I think about what had happened that might help me understand the confusing part?

QuickREFERENCE

★★★ Multicultural Link

Point out that Mr. Gumpy invites his friends for "tea." Mention that afternoon tea in England and other countries is like a snack or an early supper.
Ask children what they might say to their friends instead.

30

31

"Goodbye," said Mr. Gumpy.
"Come for a ride another day."

32

Phonemic Awareness

Producing Rhyming Words

Teach/Model

TESTED SKILL

Say these rhyming words from the story: *goat/boat*. Ask children to tell what they notice about how the words sound at the end. Then say the words again.

Think Aloud

I know that *goat* and *boat* both end with the same sounds -- *oat*. When you say the words aloud, they sound the same and rhyme. I can think of another word that rhymes with *goat* and *boat* – *float*. That word has the same end sounds too.

Practice/Apply

- Ask children to look at the picture on pages 30–31. Name the following characters and have children think of words that rhyme with them: cat, dog, boy, sheep (hat, frog, toy, beep).

Challenge Have children choose one pair of rhyming words and make pictures to illustrate both words.

SKILL FINDER Producing Rhyming Words, p. T29

2

Interact
with
Literature

Rereading

More Choices for Rereading

Choosing a Funny Scene

As children listen to the story, have them think about the funny things the animals did to help tip the boat over. Pause occasionally for children to identify those incidents and discuss what makes them funny.

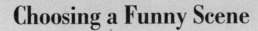

Funny Things Animals Did	
• The goat kicked	• The pig mucked about
• The calf trampled	• The dog teased the cat
• The chickens flapped	• The cat chased the rabbit
• The sheep bleated	

After finishing the story, have children take a vote on which was their favorite funny or silly part.

Act It Out

Students Acquiring English Make a large rectangle and lay it on the floor. Encourage children to pretend that this is Mr. Gumpy's boat. Invite them to act out the scenes of Mr. Gumpy, the animals, and children as they tip the boat as you reread the story. Assign individual children the various characters' parts. Before rereading, review what Mr. Gumpy had told each animal not to do. As they dramatize the scenes, they should act out what their character did to help the boat tip.

Rereading with Sound and Movement

Add sounds and movements that children can do when they hear the animals' names. For instance:

rabbit (place hands on head for bunny ears)
cat (say meow-meow)
dog (say bow-wow)
pig (squash nose upward like a pig)
sheep (say bah-bah)
chickens (flap like a chicken)
calf (trample (stomp) feet in place)
goat (kick one foot in place)

Informal Assessment

As you reread the selection note whether or not children respond to literature with questions and/or comments.

Responding

Choices for Responding

Literature Discussion

As a class, discuss the following questions:

- Do you think Mr. Gumpy's outing turned out to be what he expected? How might it have turned out differently?

- What if the animals had tried to blame each other for tipping over the boat. Whose fault would you say it was?

- What advice would you give to Mr. Gumpy and his friends if they want to go out in the boat again?

What Surprised Me

Ask children to draw and write about the part of the story that surprised them the most. Encourage them to share their work.

Home Connection

Have children draw their favorite scene from the story and write or dictate a sentence or two about it. They can use their illustration to help retell the story to a family member.

Students Acquiring English Have children draw one or more pictures of what happened in the story. Then ask them to use the pictures to retell the story at home in their primary language.

Using Story Props

Materials
- Story Retelling Props boat and figures (See Teacher's Handbook, page H2.)

Invite volunteers to use the story prop boat and figures to retell the story. Children should take turns placing figures one by one into the boat. Encourage them to recall the dialogue between Mr. Gumpy and the other characters. When all of the characters are in the boat, children will enjoy tipping them out and beginning the story again.

After the activity is completed, place the story prop boat and figures in the Reading/Listening Center for children to use independently.

Portfolio Opportunity

- You may want to videotape children retelling the selection and keep the videotape in a video portfolio.

3

Instruct and Integrate

Comprehension

Literacy Activity Book, p. 30

Practice Activities

Noting Details

LAB, p. 30

Materials
- Story Retelling Props boat and figures (See Teacher's Handbook, page H2.)

Extra Support Hold up the story boat prop. Ask children who was the first character from the story in the boat. (When they answer *Mr. Gumpy*, place this story figure in the boat.)

- Ask why it is important to remember that Mr. Gumpy was the first character in the boat. (It was his boat. It was Mr. Gumpy whom the children and all the animals asked if they could come in.)

- Have children place the next two character figures in the boat. (the two children) Ask if the boat tipped with just Mr. Gumpy and the two children in it. (no)

- Continue similarly having children add the other figures to the boat. After adding a few more figures, ask if the boat tipped then. (no)

- If children have difficulty recalling the order of the characters, refer to the illustrations in the story. Point out that since there are so many characters to remember, the pictures in this story can be very helpful.

- Finally when all the figures are in the boat, ask if the boat tipped. (yes) Explain that they might not understand why the boat tipped if they didn't remember that there were a lot of characters in the boat and that they all started to do things Mr. Gumpy told them not to do.

- Have children complete *Literacy Activity Book* page 30.

A New Idea for Mr. Gumpy

Ask children to think about what Mr. Gumpy could have done to keep his boat from tipping over. Invite children to illustrate their ideas. Have them share their drawings with others in the class.

Warning: Beware!

Have children think of the warning signs they know, such as "Do Not Enter." Draw several different kinds of signs or shapes on chart paper. Then have children draw and cut out their own signs to warn other animals what <u>not</u> to do on a boat. Have them write or dictate a sentence telling about their warning.

Informal Assessment

As children complete the activities assess their ability to note story details and produce rhyming words.

Phonemic Awareness

Practice Activities

Producing Rhyming Words

LAB, p. 31

Extra Support Read the song, "Row, Row, Row Your Boat" with children emphasizing the rhyming pair *stream/dream* as you read. After reading, say each word of the rhyming pair. Repeat the words with children and have them tell you what they hear about how the words sound.

- Have children suggest additional words that rhyme with the pair. If necessary, say a few words aloud, such as *cream* and *team,* and have children contribute others. Have children tell how the words sound similar.

- Have children complete *Literacy Activity Book* p. 31.

Literacy Activity Book, p. 31

Don't Tip the Boat

- Have children recall the names of the animals in the story and the things they liked to do that Mr. Gumpy asked them not to do in the boat.

- Have children make a list of other animals and the things they like to do that would not be a good idea in a boat.

Not Good in a Boat	
frog	hop up and down
porcupine	shake its fur full of needles
seal	flap its flippers
mule	kick and say hee-haw, hee-haw

Children might enjoy illustrating a funny scene in which some of these animals are in Mr. Gumpy's boat.

Guess My Animal

Pairs can create an animal guessing game. Ask them to choose four animal pictures and put them in an envelope. To play the game, one child draws a picture but doesn't show it to the other player. He or she just gives clues such as the sound the animal makes, what it looks like, or what its name rhymes with. If the listener guesses correctly, he or she keeps the picture.

Students Acquiring English Have children acquiring English play this game in pairs with native speakers.

Portfolio Opportunity

Save *Literacy Activity Book* page 31 to have a record of children's ability to identify rhyming words. Also keep their work from A New Idea or Warning: Beware! as a record of their comprehension.

3
Instruct *and* Integrate

Oral Language

Choices for Oral Language

Home Connection

Invite children to bring in and share with the class pictures, postcards, and other mementos of outings they have shared with family and friends. Set aside time each day for a week for different children to share their outings with the class.

Action! Action!

Students Acquiring English Read aloud page 24, emphasizing the action words with your voice. Invite children to demonstrate what *flap* means. Then ask them to demonstrate what they think *chased* means. Continue in this manner by encouraging children to perform each action mentioned in the story.

Traveling Words

Recall with children that the story is called *Mr. Gumpy's Outing*. Discuss with children what an "outing" is. Encourage them to think of words that mean the same thing or almost the same thing, such as *picnic, trip, journey, ride, hike,* and *drive*. You might record their ideas in a word web. Encourage them to use the words in oral sentences.

Name It or Do It

Children can play a game in which they identify action words.

- Ask children to listen for a word that tells something you can do: *book, cat, jump.*

- Then have them identify action words in each of the following sets of words: *boat, kick, pig; hop, river, house.*

- Read different pages of *Mr. Gumpy's Outing* and have children pick out the word that means something that can be done.

- Have children work with partners to plan and act out one word. The audience can guess what the word is.

Informal Assessment

- As children complete the oral language/vocabulary activities note whether they exhibit good vocabulary and speak in complete sentences.

- As children work on their writing assignments, note their ability to express their ideas.

Writing

Choices for Writing

Tea Party Menu

Tell children to imagine they were going to a tea party. What foods would they like to eat at the party? Give each child a white paper plate. Have them either cut pictures from magazines and paste them onto the plate or draw the foods on colored paper and paste them on. Encourage them to include a variety of foods of different colors. Then have them write or dictate the colors and names next to the foods on their plate. Children can sit around a table and share the foods they drew for the tea party.

Challenge Invite children to work in pairs and write invitations for their tea party. Help them decide what information is important to include. (time, date, place, name of person they're inviting) Then have them design a card and write or dictate what they would like to say on it.

A Favorite Outing

Ask children to tell about a trip they have taken or would like to take. Children may want to tell about something funny or silly that may have happened on their trip. Invite them to draw a picture of themselves going on an outing to a favorite place. Have children write, or dictate, a sentence about their drawings.

Challenge Bring in brochures and pamphlets from other countries. Invite children to draw a place they would like to visit. Have them write or dictate a sentence telling why they want to visit.

A Silly Animal

Give children drawing paper and a variety of materials, such as buttons, tissue paper, and bits of yarn to create an imaginary animal that could go for a ride in Mr. Gumpy's boat. Invite children to name their animals and to tell what their animals would do to cause the boat to tip. Have them write or dictate sentences about their creations. Display their work on a bulletin board to be shared.

Portfolio Opportunity

Save children's Favorite Outing picture as a record of their ability to convey meaning.

3
Instruct *and* Integrate

Cross-Curricular Activities

Music

A New Verse

Have children use the tune and language of "Old MacDonald Had a Farm" to create new verses for "Mr. Gumpy Had a Boat." Help children get started with the following verse and see if they can add other verses.

> Mr. Gumpy had a boat.
> E, I, E, I, O.
> And on his boat there was a pig.
> E, I, E, I, O.
> With an oink, oink, here and an oink, oink, there.
> Here an oink, there an oink, everywhere an oink, oink.
> Mr. Gumpy had a boat.
> E, I, E, I, O.

Art

Styrofoam Boats

Recall with children that the characters in the story all traveled in Mr. Gumpy's boat. Invite them to make their own boats. Provide styrofoam trays for the boats, craft sticks for the oars, and a variety of materials for decorating the vessels. If possible, fill a water table for children to float their boats in.

Challenge Have children place objects on their boats as they float in water to find out whether the boats will tip or sink with each new addition.

Math

Passenger Count

Reread the story so children can count the number of characters that travel with Mr. Gumpy in his boat. Each time a new passenger comes aboard, ask a child to make a tally mark on the chalkboard. Then help children count the tally marks to discover the number of passengers Mr. Gumpy has on his boat at the end of the story.

Challenge Have children stack a unifix cube for each tally mark and count the number of characters again using the cubes.

Social Studies

Aye-Aye Captain!

Discuss with children the many people that are needed to run a ship and what their jobs are.

Invite them to role-play the different workers on the ship. You might also teach them the words to the following song that they can sing on board their ship:

A sailor went to sea, sea, sea,
To see what he could see, see, see.
And all that he could see, see, see,
Was the middle of the deep blue sea, sea, sea.

Captain	person in charge of the ship
First mate	second in command
Navigator	steers the boat
Engineer	makes sure engines are working
Deckhands	keeps the ship in working order

BIG BOOK
SELECTION:
Ten Black Dots

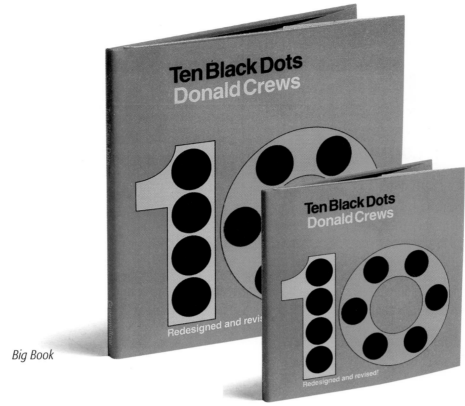

Big Book

Little Big Book

by Donald Crews

Other Books by the Author

School Bus

Bicycle Race

Freight Train

● **Best Books for Children**

Selection Summary

This counting book in rhyme introduces number concepts. Numbers of black dots or circles from 1–10 are shown as parts of objects, such as a fox's eyes, beads for a stringing on a lace, and wheels to a train. Children learn number sense through words, numerals, and pictures and think about the many places they can see dots!

Lesson Planning Guide

	Skill/Strategy Instruction	Meeting Individual Needs	Lesson Resources
1 **Introduce** *the* **Literature** *Pacing: 1 day*	**Shared Reading and Writing** Warm-up/Build Background, T36 Shared Reading, T36 Shared Writing, T37	Choices for Rereading, T37	**Poster** Yesterday's Paper, T36 *Literacy Activity Book* Personal Response, p. 32
2 **Interact** *with* **Literature** *Pacing: 1–2 days*	**Reading Strategies** Predict/Infer, T38 Think About Words, T40 Summarize, T46 Evaluate, T50, T52 **Minilessons** Numeral Identification, T41 ✔ Sequence, T43 ✔ Spoken Word as Word, T45 Number/Object Equivalents 1–10, T47 Return Sweep, T51 Adding 1 to the Numbers 1-9, T53	**Students Acquiring English,** T39, T48, T49 **Extra Support,** T40, T54 **Challenge,** T41, T44, T53 **Rereading and Responding,** T54–T55	**Story Props,** T55 *Literacy Activity Book* Language Patterns, p. 33 **Audio Tape** for Just for Fun: *Ten Black Dots* See the Houghton Mifflin **Internet** resources for additional activities.
3 **Instruct** *and* **Integrate** *Pacing: 1–2 days*	**Reading/Listening Center** Comprehension, T56 Concept Development, T57 Concepts About Print, T58 Listening, T59 **Language/Writing Center** Oral Language, T60 Writing, T61 **Cross-Curricular Center** Cross-Curricular Activities, T62-T63	**Challenge,** T57, T59 **Extra Support,** T56, T58, T60	**Poster** Numbers Everywhere!, T60 Number Shapes, T62 **Story Props,** T62 *My Big Dictionary,* T57 *Literacy Activity Book* Comprehension, p. 34 Concept Development, p. 35 See the Houghton Mifflin **Internet** resources for additional activities.

✔ *Indicates Tested Skills. See page T11 for assessment options.*

Introduce *the* Literature

Shared Reading and Writing

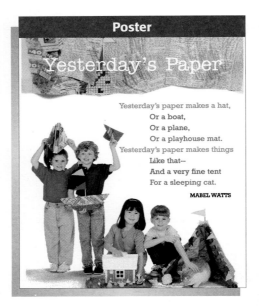

Poster

Yesterday's Paper

Yesterday's paper makes a hat,
Or a boat,
Or a plane,
Or a playhouse mat.
Yesterday's paper makes things
Like that--
And a very fine tent
For a sleeping cat.

MABEL WATTS

INTERACTIVE LEARNING

Warm-up/ Building Background

Sharing a Poem

Invite children to listen and follow along as you read aloud the poem "Yesterday's Paper." Reread the poem again inviting children to raise their hand when you name something they would like to make and play with from an old newspaper.

Discuss the poem by asking:

- How can a newspaper be a boat? A plane? A tent?

- Can you think of anything you could make using a newspaper?

- Have you ever used one thing to make another thing?

- Take a sheet of newspaper and cut a large circle out of it. Hold it up and ask children to name the shape you made.

- Ask them what they could make with this paper circle. (Examples: wheel, place mat, sun, face mask)

- Explain that in the story you will read, they will see circles of all sizes, which are called dots. Children may be surprised at how many different things these dots can be.

Shared Reading

LAB, p. 32

Preview and Predict

- Display the cover of *Ten Black Dots* and read the title and author/illustrator's name.

- Take a picture walk through the first few pages.

- Ask children where the circles, which are all called dots, seem to be in the illustrations. Have them tell what they think they might learn about numbers and dots in this book.

Read Together

Read the story aloud as children listen. Pause and allow children to count the dots on each spread after you read the text. Then show them the corresponding number in the text for the amount they name.

After reading, give children a chance to discuss whether they were surprised by what they learned in the book. If they made predictions, have them comment on whether or not their ideas about the dots were correct.

Personal Response

Invite children to tell you what they liked best about the story. Then have them complete *Literacy Activity Book* page 32.

 ## Shared Writing: *A Class Counting Book*

Brainstorming

- Have children brainstorm other shapes they could use to count from one to ten. Draw their ideas on chart paper, and have them choose their favorite one.

- Next, write the numbers 1–5 on the chart paper. Have children say the numbers as you point to each one.

- Remind them that in *Ten Black Dots*, the author used one dot to make a sun. Have children suggest ways they could use the shape they chose to show the number 5.

- Write their ideas in the chart for each number.

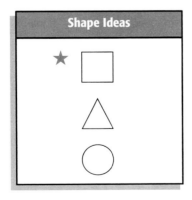

Drafting

Assign groups of children one of the five numbers. For each group, give them cut outs of the shape. Have each group illustrate the number they were given using the shapes. (Example: Group 2 uses 2 squares to make a robot.) Have them write or dictate a sentence about the concept and number.

Publishing

Have each group present their page and tell the number, show its' representation in the illustration, and read their sentence. When all five have been presented, help children put the book together to keep in the Reading/Listening Center.

Choices for Rereading

Rereadings enable children to focus on different aspects of a story and to respond to it in varying ways. You may want to use some or all of the rereading choices on page T54

- Listen and Read
- Creating a Language Pattern
- Rhyme Time
- Keeping Count with Number Cards

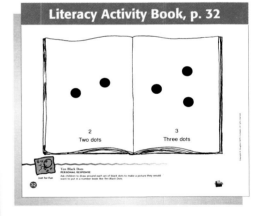
Literacy Activity Book, p. 32

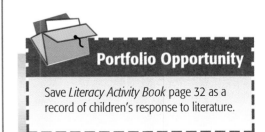
Portfolio Opportunity

Save *Literacy Activity Book* page 32 as a record of children's response to literature.

Interact *with* **Literature**

Reading Strategies

▶ **Predict/Infer**

Discussion Remind children that when they listened to this story the first time, they thought about what they might learn about dots. They made guesses and then listened to the story to see if they were right.

Tell them that as they listen to the book again, they can think about what else the author might have used to show the numbers.

1One dot can make a sun

4

What
can
you do
with
ten
black
dots?

3

or a moon
when day
is done.

QuickREFERENCE

Visual Literacy

Have children look at the details in the pictures on pages 4 and 5. Ask them how the illustrator shows that the sun is shining brightly and what else he includes with the moon to show that it is a night sky.

 Students Acquiring English

MEETING INDIVIDUAL NEEDS

Pair students with partners for support. Together they might look through the pictures to identify the numerals and count the dots in each illustration.

Interact *with* Literature

Reading Strategies

▶ **Think About Words**

Reread pages 8 and 9, pausing when you get to the word lace. Ask children to predict the word you will read. Discuss the following:

- **What makes sense** The three dots are beads. Beads can be used for many things, like a necklace. You string beads on a necklace, so it must be something used to put the beads on.

- **Picture clues** The beads are being strung on a shoelace. Sometimes people say lace as a short way of saying shoelace. You could string beads on a lace to make a necklace.

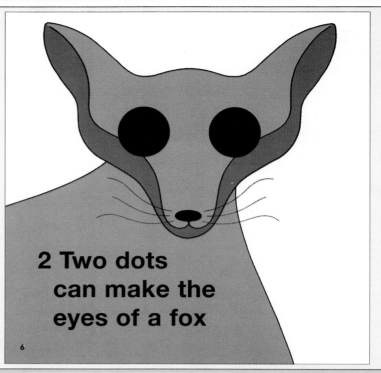

2 Two dots can make the eyes of a fox

6

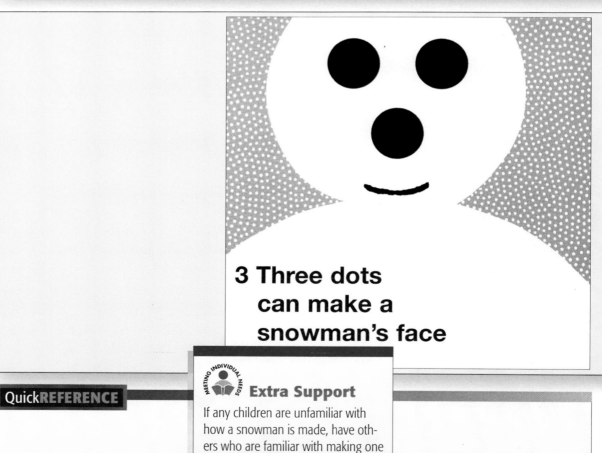

3 Three dots can make a snowman's face

QuickREFERENCE

Extra Support

If any children are unfamiliar with how a snowman is made, have others who are familiar with making one explain the steps for building a snowman.

**or the eyes
of keys that
open locks.**

7

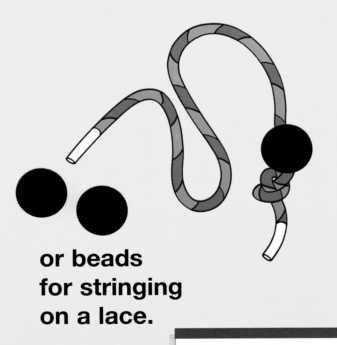

**or beads
for stringing
on a lace.**

Concept Development

Numeral Identification

Teach/Model

Point out the numeral 2 on page 6. Remind children that the number is the very first thing you read on each page in this counting book.

Think Aloud

I know that just like letters and words, I can read the numbers in this book. So far, I read the numbers 1, 2, and 3. I also know that the title is *Ten Black Dots,* so I'll probably read more numbers and they may go all the way to 10!

Practice/Apply

Invite children to look back at pages 4 - 9 and have volunteers point to and identify the numerals 1 -3. Then together with children, page through the book to page 27, identifying the numerals when they occur.

SKILL FINDER — Number Match; Numerals and Numbers, p. T57

Challenge

Point out that the beads are strung on a shoe lace. Challenge children to think of other things they could string on a shoe lace or other things they could use a shoe lace for.

Vocabulary

Help children understand that the "eye" of the key is the hole. Pass a key around so all children can see and identify the eye, which is used to hang the key on a key chain.

BIG BOOK

**4 Four dots
can make seeds from
which flowers grow**

10

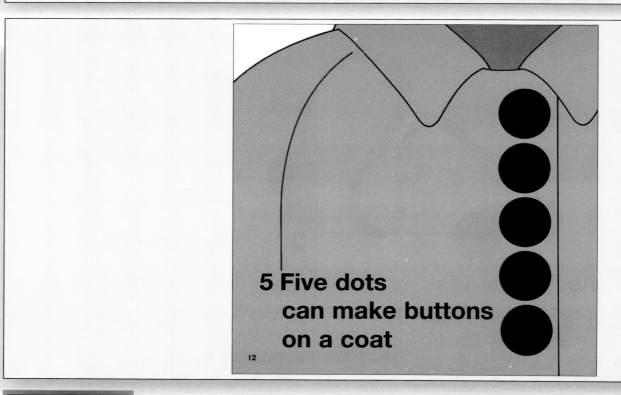

**5 Five dots
can make buttons
on a coat**

12

QuickREFERENCE

Science Link

Invite children to tell about any seeds that they have seen. Ask them why the author uses dots for seeds.

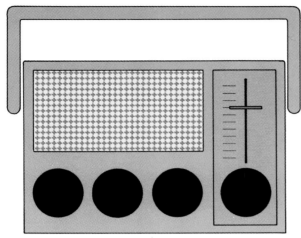

**or the
knobs on
a radio.**

11

**or the
portholes
of a boat.**

Comprehension

Sequence

TESTED SKILL

Teach/Model

Explain that the numbers in this counting book are in order starting with the number one, then two, three and so on up to ten. Point out that knowing that numbers follow an order can help them figure out what might happen next as they listen to and read books.

Think Aloud

So far, I have learned about things with one dot, two dots, three dots, and then four dots. I know that five comes after four so I wonder if the next page will be about things with five dots.

Practice/Apply

Have children read pages 11 and 12 together with you and then ask volunteers to count the number of dots in each of the illustrations. Then ask children to predict the number of dots that will be found when you turn the page.

SKILL FINDER

Number Sequence, p. T56

Minilessons, see Themes 1; 7; 8; 11

Media Literacy

Display a radio and have children point out the knobs. During free time, have children listen to the radio and talk about whether they or people in their family listen to the radio.

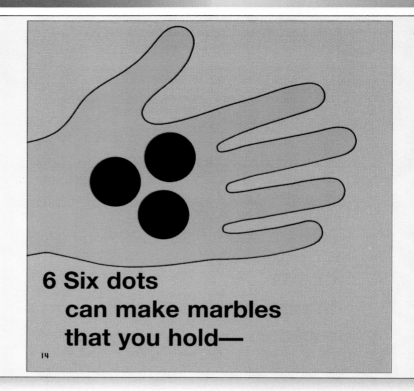

**6 Six dots
can make marbles
that you hold—**

14

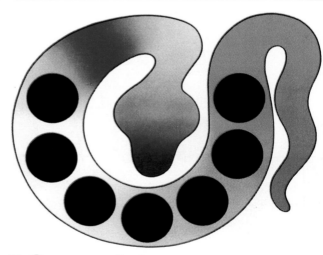

**7 Seven dots
can make the spots
on a snake**

QuickREFERENCE

Math Link

To help children understand the concept of dividing six marbles in half, give pairs of children six counters. Ask them to decide on a fair way to share the objects or food. Once divided equally, point out that each child has half or three each.

Challenge

MEETING INDIVIDUAL NEEDS

Invite children to look at pages 10 and 16. Ask them to tell which page has more dots. How can they tell?

**half are
new, the rest
are old.**

15

**or stones
turned up by a
garden rake.**

Concepts About Print

Spoken Word As Word

TESTED SKILL

Teach/Model

Tell children that when we speak, it's a good idea to speak slowly so that others can understand what we're saying. Model this for them.

Think Aloud

When I read the story with you, I have to be careful to speak slowly. If I had said (run words together) *spotsonasnake,* you might have thought that I was saying one big word that you didn't know. Instead, I had to speak slowly so you could hear and understand the four words *spots on a snake.*

Practice/Apply

Say the following phrases slowly and have children repeat each one after you and tell how many words they said: *the eyes of a fox; keys that open locks; marbles that you hold; the rest are old.*

SKILL FINDER Spoken Word As Word, p. T58

Science Link

Have children think of other shapes they see on a snake, such as stripes or diamond patterns. Discuss the different kinds of snakes that children have seen or know about.

Review

Days of the Week Point out a class calendar. Ask children if they know why the number seven is especially important on a calendar. (There are seven days in a week.) Ask children to count and name the seven days on the calendar.

Interact *with* Literature

Reading Strategies

▶ **Summarizing**

Remind children that remembering the important parts of a story help them remember what the story was about. Ask them if they remember all of the numbers and pictures so far. Have volunteers summarize the number and concept idea for numbers 1-8. If children have trouble recalling a number or object, reread the page(s) with them.

8 Eight dots can make the wheels of a train

18

9 Nine dots can make toy soldiers standing in rank

20

QuickREFERENCE

Science Link

As children look at the train on pages 18 and 19, invite them to categorize other things that move on wheels, such as buses, cars, bicycles, wagons, or roller skates.

carrying freight through sun and rain.

19

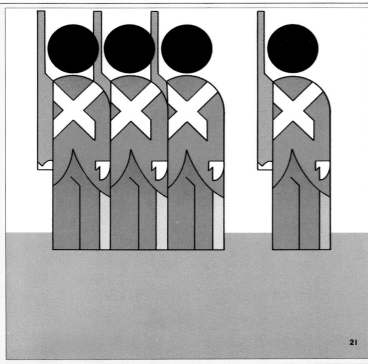

21

Vocabulary

Demonstrate the word freight by placing blocks in the car of a toy train. Explain that the things the train carries from one place to another is called *freight*. Have children tell what kinds of things a train might carry.

Concept Development
Number/Object Equivalents (1–10)

Teach/Model

Point to the numeral 8 on page 18. Have children say the number 8 with you. Explain that 8 is the name of this number, and it tells how many dots make the wheels of the train.

Think Aloud

I know that when I see the number 8 here that the picture will show 8 dots. I can count them — one, two, three, four, five, six, seven, eight dots are wheels on the train.

Practice/Apply

- Have children turn back to pages 8. Ask them to name the numeral 3 and find three dots on the snowman's face.

- Give children three dots and a piece of paper. Have them make a face and write the number three to show number/object equivalency.

SKILL FINDER Number Match; Numerals and Numbers, p. T57

Interact *with* **Literature**

or the pennies
in your
piggy bank.

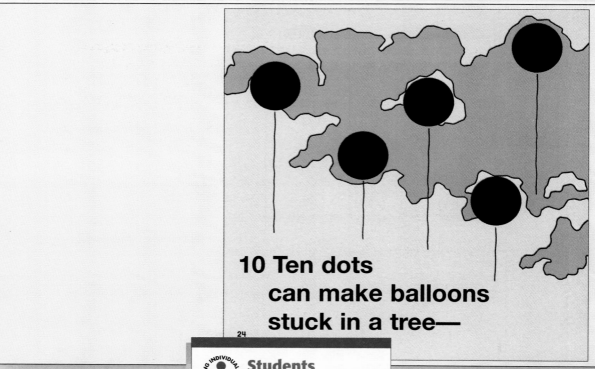

10 Ten dots
can make balloons
stuck in a tree—

24

QuickREFERENCE

Math Link

Invite children to count the pennies in the piggy bank on pages 22 and 23. Then have volunteers drop nine pennies into a jar or other container and count as they do it.

Students Acquiring English

MEETING INDIVIDUAL NEEDS

Second-language speakers may not be familiar with *piggy banks.* If possible, display a piggy bank and invite children to show how it is used.

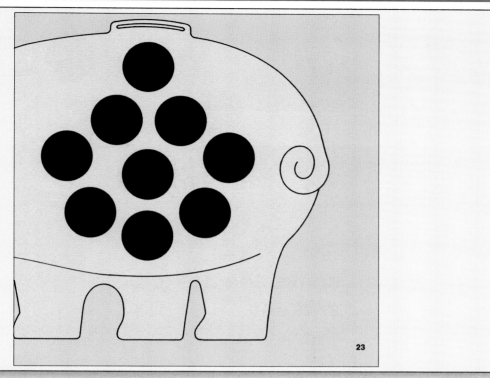

23

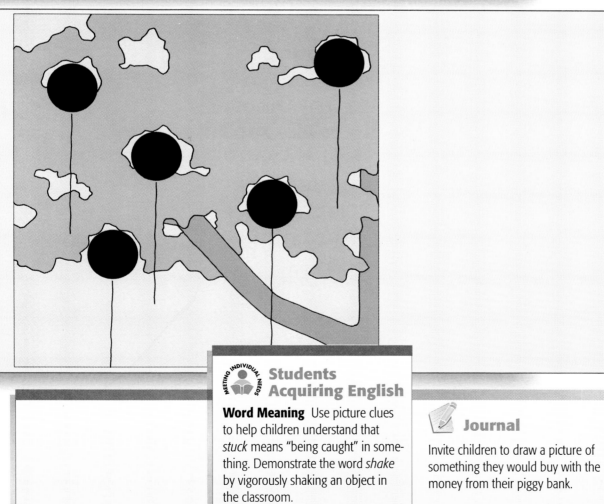

Journal

Invite children to draw a picture of something they would buy with the money from their piggy bank.

Interact with Literature

Reading Strategies

▶ **Evaluate**

Have children explain what happened to the ten black dots at the end of the book. Ask if they think this was a good way to end this counting book and to tell why. Invite them to think of another interesting ending.

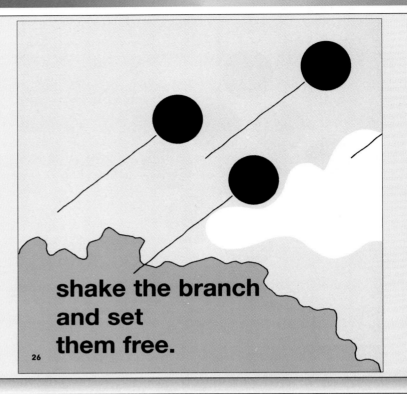

shake the branch and set them free.

26

Count them. Are there really ten? Now we can begin again, counting dots from one to ten.

28

QuickREFERENCE

Math Link
Have children look at the chart of dots on pages 28–29. Ask if they can find a number that tells how old they were when they started school this year.

Music Link
Invite children to share some counting songs they know. Then play or sing a counting song for children, and encourage them to sing along.

Review
Letter as Letter Display the letter card *t*. Point to each word as you read page 28. Have volunteers tell when they see the letter *t* in a word. Follow the same procedure for other letters in words on this page.

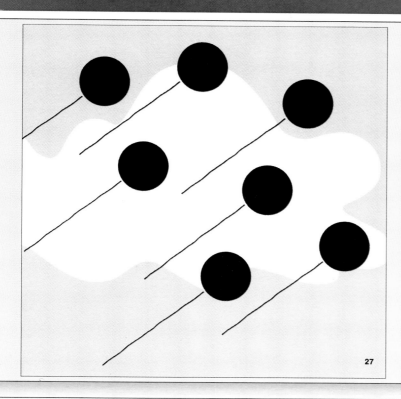

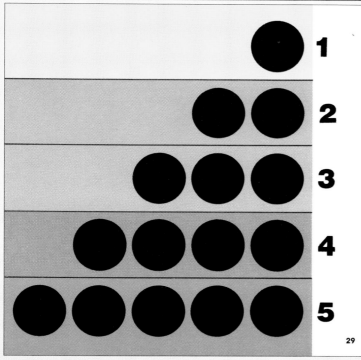

Concepts About Print

Return Sweep

Teach/Model

- Display page 28. Ask a volunteer to point to the first word they should read and have everyone point to *Count*.

- Ask another volunteer to show which word they should read next. Point out that since *Count* was the only word on the first line, the next word they read is them.

- Continue similarly with the rest of the words on the page, pointing out that since there are two words in line three, they read the word to the left *Are* first and then the word *there*.

Practice/Apply

- Have children take turns leading the class in identifying the lines and word order in subsequent lines on page 28.

 SKILL FINDER Minilessons, see Theme 2

Interact *with* Literature

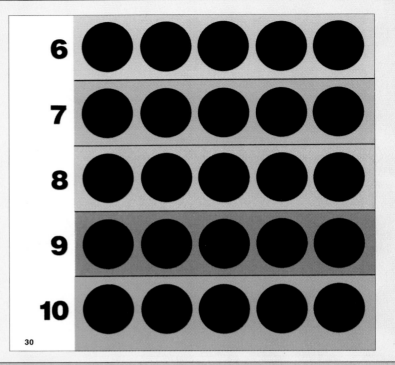

Reading Strategies

▶ **Evaluate**

Ask children to tell about other counting books with which they are familiar. Discuss how this counting book is like and different from others. Invite children to tell what they found interesting and fun about *Ten Black Dots.*

Encourage children to think about their reading by asking themselves these questions:

- Have I been looking for the important parts of the story? What important information have I found?
- Have I asked myself if I am understanding the story? What did I do if I didn't understand something.

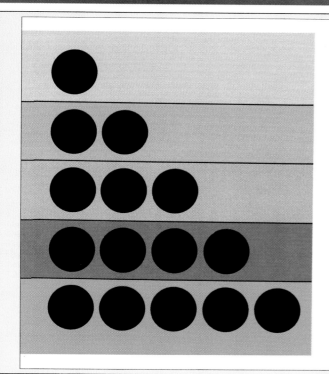

31

Concept Development

Adding 1 to the Numbers 1-9

Teach/Model

Hold up a dot that has been cut from colored paper and is the same size as the ones in the chart on pages 29 - 31. Ask children how many dots you are holding. (one) Place it over the dot next to the number 1. Point out that this counting book starts with the number one, and keeps adding one dot to each row until there are ten dots. Demonstrate and model how one is added to each number.

Think Aloud

I know that if I place this one dot on the next line in the chart I add my one dot to another dot. That makes two dots. Then if I move the dot down, I add my dot to two dots to make three. For each number, if I add my one dot I will get another number. I can do this all the way until I have the number 10.

Practice/Apply

- Give children their own set of ten large dots. Have them start by placing one dot in front of them. Then as a group, have them add a dot and count the new number with them.

- Continue similarly with all ten dots.

MEETING INDIVIDUAL NEEDS
Challenge

Incorporate counting by one in other activities throughout the day:
- Have ten children line up by "ones."
- Ask each child to put away ten of something and as they do to count one by one.

Interact with Literature

Rereading

Literacy Activity Book, p. 33

1 One dot can make a

2 Two dots can make

3 Three dots can make

4 Four dots can make

Ten Black Dots
LANGUAGE PATTERNS

Just for Fun

Ask children to identify the rebus pictures at the end of the first two sentences (bee, keys). Then read these sentences aloud. Read each number word on the lines, having children trace the numeral and the word to repeat the language pattern from the selection. Read the incomplete sentences with children and invite them to draw a picture at the end of each one to complete it.

33

Choices for Rereading

Rhyme Time

Tell children to listen for two rhyming words as you read each two-page spread. On some pages, pause to point out the words that rhyme and contain the same rhyming letters. Have children name the letters in both words that make the rhyming sound.

Creating a Language Pattern

LAB, p.33

- Ask children to follow along and chime in as you read pages 2 through 7.

- Have them identify the pattern in the text: the repeating phrase, _____ *dots can make* _____.

- Remind children that this is a pattern that is used throughout the book.

- Encourage them to join in on this phrase as you finish rereading the book.

- Then ask children how they might make a new pattern using _____ *dots can make* _____. Write their suggestions on the board or chart paper.

- Have children complete *Literacy Activity Book* p. 33.

Keeping Count with Number Cards

Distribute teacher-made number cards 1–10 to pairs of children. As you reread the story, pause after reading each spread. Partners should put down the correct number card for the number you just finished reading about. At the end, have children count the number cards 1–10 together.

Listen and Read!

Audio Tape for Just for Fun: *Ten Black Dots*

Extra Support Children can listen to the Audio Tape and follow along in the Little Big Book of *Ten Black Dots*. Provide children independent reading opportunities by placing the tape along with books in the Reading/Listening Center.

Informal Assessment

Choose from the Responding Activities to assess children's general understanding of the story.

Additional Support:

- Have children use the story props to retell *Ten Black Dots* in their own words.

- Have children orally answer the question: *What can you do with ten black dots?* which is the question asked on the first page of the book.

Responding

Choices for Responding

Personal Response

Ask children to think about all of the interesting ways the author and illustrator used dots. Have them draw a picture of their favorite part in the story. Suggest that if they can't remember the number of dots they should include to ask you or consult the book. They can write or dictate a sentence telling about their picture.

Literature Discussion

Divide the class into small groups and have them use a copy of the Little Big Book. Ask them as a group to decide on their favorite set of pages about one number. Have one spokesperson from each group share the pages they chose and tell why. Include the following in discussion:

- This book is in a theme called "Just For Fun." What makes this book fun?
- How is this book different from other counting books you have read?
- What did you learn from reading this book?

Numbers and Dots

Materials
- Story Prop Dot Cards

Use the dot cards in several different activities:

- Display the cards. Ask volunteers to choose one and count aloud how many dots there are on the card.
- Mix the cards and have children try to put the dots in order by number.
- Have children draw something with a given number of dots. Let them use the card to copy the number of dots they chose onto their pictures.

Home Connection Ask children to brainstorm with a partner some things that they find around their home that have the shape of a circle or has a circle in it. Then have them draw one of these things and write or dictate a sentence telling about it.

Instruct
and
Integrate

Comprehension

Practice Activities

Number Sequence

LAB, p. 34

MEETING INDIVIDUAL NEEDS

Extra Support Tell children that when they count, they go in a certain order. Since numbers follow a certain order, it is easy to tell if they forget a number or if a number is missing.

- Invite one child to stand alone to represent 1.

- Form other groups for 2, 3, 4, and 5. These groups should stand in a straight row an arm's length apart. Have the class name how many are in each group.

- Do the same procedure but place the three group after the one group.

- Ask children to point out and describe what is wrong. Help them to articulate that knowing the order numbers go in helped them to figure out that the groups were in the wrong order.

- Have children complete *Literacy Activity Book* page 34.

What Number Will Come Next?

Remind children that *Ten Black Dots* is a counting book and that counting books follow the special order of numbers.

- Invite a volunteer up to the Big Book and open it to a spread. Reread the pages with children. Then invite volunteers to predict what number will come next in the story.

- Turn the page to check their predictions.

- Repeat the procedure with other story pages.

Order the Numbers

Invite pairs to place the numeral cards in order in a row. Then ask them to make sets of counters to show each number. Have pairs use copies of the Little Big Book *Ten Black Dots* to check the sequence of their cards and sets.

Materials
- Teacher-made numeral cards one through ten
- counters

Informal Assessment

As children work through the activities, note whether they understand the sequence of numbers one through ten.

Concept Development

Practice Activities

Reviewing *Aa* Through *Mm*

Display the cover and remind children that *My Big Dictionary* shows all the letters of the alphabet. Turn to page 2. Have a volunteer identify capital *A* and small *a*. Then ask children to look at the illustration and name the objects they see that begin with the letter *a*. Follow this procedure for the letters *b* through *m*.

What Color Balloon?

Give children a pattern for a balloon made out of construction paper. Tell them to color the balloon one of these colors — whichever they like best: blue, green, yellow, or red. Give them a ribbon to attach to the balloon and let them hang their balloons on a class display by color. Then have children count the number of balloons in each color category to see which color was the class favorite. You could also show the results in a graph.

Number Match

Challenge Have small groups of children play a game of number match. Provide each child with a chart similar to the one on page 29 of *Ten Black Dots*, but provide only outlines for dots. Children will color them in. To play:

- One child rolls the die and counts the number of dots.

- He/she colors the column of dots that match the number on the die.

- The first child to color in all five numbers wins.

Materials
- chart for each child
- die for each group of children
- crayons

Numerals and Numbers

LAB, p. 35

- Write the numerals 1, 2, and 3 as headings on a chart.

- Ask children to find things on themselves or in the room for each of these numbers.

- Help them to count the objects and then draw pictures showing the things under the numerals 1, 2, and 3 on the chart.

- Have children complete *Literacy Activity Book* page 35.

Home Connection Encourage children to take the page home to share with their families.

Literacy Activity Book, p. 35

My Big Dictionary

Portfolio Opportunity

Save *Literacy Activity Book* page 34 to have a record of children's ability to identify the numerals one through ten.

3

Instruct *and* Integrate

Concepts About Print

Practice Activities

Concentration

Have children play a game of concentration.

- Make 20 balloon or other shape cards out of oak tag.

- Make a numeral and a word card for the numbers 1–10. Example: on one balloon write the numeral (1). On another, write the word (one) and one dot. (Children may not be able to read the word, but they can count the dots and see the number/word equivalent.)

- Place the twenty balloons face down in random order.

- Children take turns picking two cards. They get a match and keep the cards when both the numeral and the word for a number match.

- The player with the most cards at the end of the game wins.

Spoken Word As Word

Extra Support Say each of the following sentences slowly so that you pause briefly between words. After each one, have children tell how many words you said:

    Good morning.
    I am hungry.
    This is good.
    Yes.

Have children take turns speaking sentences slowly while others tell how many words each is saying.

Creating New Verses

Reread the book and cover the right hand pages. Ask for volunteers to come up with a different object and a rhyme to go with the left hand page.

Informal Assessment

As children complete the Listening activities note their ability to identify individual words in a stream of language and rhyming words.

Listening

Practice Activities

What Rhymes?

Ask children to listen for rhyming words as you say the rhyme:

> One, two, buckle my shoe.
> Three, four, shut the door.
> Five, six, pick up sticks.
> Seven, eight, lay them straight.
> Nine, ten, big fat hen.

Materials
- teacher-made number cards 2, 4, 6, 8, 10
- teacher-made picture cards of a shoe, door, stick, hen

- Place the number cards along the chalkboard ledge or in a pocket chart. Leave room between each for children to place a picture card. Have children read the numbers with you.

- Reread the rhyme and have volunteers place the picture card next to the number it rhymes with. Discuss and possibly add a picture that children think of for number eight.

- Challenge children to think of other words that rhyme with each pair.

Word Toss

Play a rhyming game with children standing in a circle. Toss a ball to a child and say a word, such as *cat.* The child says a rhyming word, such as *hat* as he or she catches the ball. The child then throws the ball back and the play continues using different one-syllable known rhyming words such as: *ball, cat, sit, Jack, hot,* and *big.* Vary the game by rolling the ball, hopping, or clapping each time a rhyming word is spoken.

Giant Steps

Have children play a version of "Mother May I" using a big black dot as the finish line. Children stand in a row facing the leader. Each child takes a turn asking the leader whether he or she can take a certain number of giant steps. The child must include "May I" in the question or he or she loses a turn. The first child to reach the big dot wins.

Challenge Have the leader say a word. Each child must say a word that rhymes with the leader's word in order to advance one step. The first child to reach the big dot wins.

3

Instruct
and
Integrate

Oral Language

Choices for Oral Language

Saving Those Pennies

Nine pennies went into a piggy bank. Some children may have a piggy bank where they save their own money. Have children discuss why it is a good idea to save money. They might think about such things as:

- What they could save for
- How much different things cost
- How they could earn money to save
- Where they can keep money they have saved
- How they can keep track of how much money they have saved

Poster

Numbers **Everywhere!**

Poster: Just for Fun

Numbers Everywhere!

Display the "Numbers Everywhere!" poster and help children to identify the various places or items with numbers pictured. Then encourage them to talk about other places they see numbers.

Extra Support You may want to take the class on a walk through various classrooms, the cafeteria, or offices in your building to look for numbers. Then have volunteers share where they saw numbers.

Word Clues

Begin a game of Clue. Tell children you are thinking of something in *Ten Black Dots.* Give two clues and have a volunteer find the page and name what you are thinking of. Use clues such as the following:

- It is an animal with fur and four legs. (fox)
- They are very tiny and grow into something big and beautiful. (seeds)
- It carries freight and people and floats on water. (boat)

Invite children to give clues and choose others to search in the book for the answers.

Informal Assessment

As children complete the activities, note whether they express ideas clearly and relate comments to topics. Also observe whether children are trying to label or write about their drawings.

 # Writing

Choices for Writing

A Dot of a Different Color

Pass out colored dots of different sizes. Have children think about how the book would have been different if the dots weren't black, but were of all different colors. Challenge them to think of new ideas for the numbers using colored dots. They can draw a picture of their idea and write or dictate sentences telling about it.

What Else Do You See?

Have children imagine that they are in one of the illustrations in *Ten Black Dots*. Maybe they are taking a ride on the boat, holding the key that opens something magical, or it is their coat with the five black dots. Have them first brainstorm a list of possible writing ideas for the illustration. Then have them illustrate their ideas and write or dictate sentences telling about their illustration.

Animals with Spots

In *Ten Black Dots,* seven dots make the spots on a snake. Have children name other animals with spots. Record their suggestions in a word web. Then ask them to draw seven spots on one of the animals and label their drawing. Children may want to compile their drawings into a book titled *Animals with Spots.*

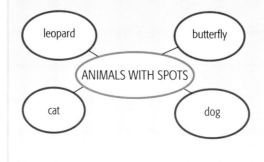

leopard — butterfly — ANIMALS WITH SPOTS — cat — dog

 **Portfolio Opportunity**

Save a writing sample from one of these activities to help you evaluate children's writing behaviors.

3

Instruct *and* **Integrate**

Cross-Curricular Activities

Poster

Math

Number Shapes!

Write the numerals one through ten on the chalkboard and encourage children to note the similarities and differences between the numeral shapes. Then display the Number Shapes poster and invite volunteers to identify the numeral shape in each photograph.

Music

Musical Numbers

Matching numerals and numbers of dots to the tune of "Where Is Thumpkin?" is a fun way to help children remember number concepts.

Distribute cards and have a class sing-along as children holding the cards respond to the lines in the song.

Teacher: *Where is 1? Where is 1?* (Child with number card for one stands and sings *Here I am. Here I am.*)

Teacher: *Can you hold up one dot? Can you hold up one dot?* (Child with dot card for one stands and sings *Yes, I can. Yes, I can.*)

Follow the same procedure for the other numbers.

Materials
- teacher-made number cards from 1–10
- Story Prop Dot Cards

Science

Water Dots

Give small groups of children a square of waxed paper. Add food coloring to color water and fill eye dropper. Place a water droplet from the eye dropper onto the paper. Tell children to be careful not to let the dot slip off the waxed paper.

Materials
- food coloring
- water
- salad oil
- liquid detergent
- eye dropper
- waxed paper

- Have children tell how this dot is the same and different from the dots in the book.

- Ask them to share ways to move the dot across the waxed paper.

- Have them talk about why the water drop didn't soak through the paper.

Add more water dots to the paper. Combine with detergent, or salad oil to see how these combinations interact with each other. Have children discuss what they observe.

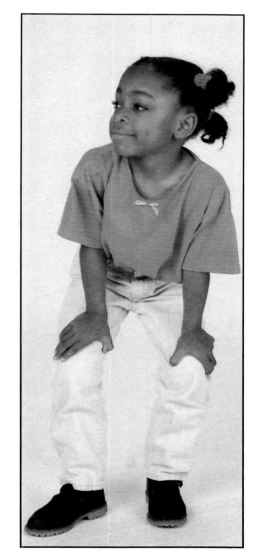

Art

Creative Creations

Working with a partner, children take a certain number of one-inch construction paper circles or squares and glue them randomly on a piece of large construction paper. Then tell children to look at the shape designs and think about how they might be used as part of a picture. To help children think about their own picture, use one pair's paper and have the class brainstorm ideas. Then have individual pairs brainstorm their own ideas. Children can use crayons, markers, or collage materials to create a picture. Invite them to share what they have made.

BIG BOOK

SELECTION:

Ten in a Bed

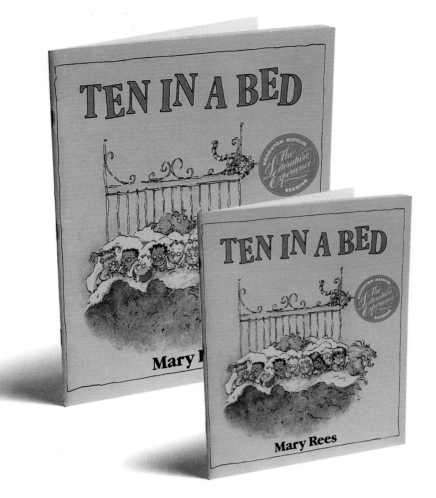

by Mary Rees

● **Best Books for Children**

Selection Summary

This is a humorous version of the well-known traditional song "Ten in a Bed". The story begins with ten children in a bed. When the little one says "Roll over! Roll over!" someone falls out. The cumulative verse continues until there is just one in the bed. The ending offers a new twist when the little one says she's not getting up, and all the overnight guests make her get up.

Lesson Planning Guide

	Skill/Strategy Instruction	Meeting Individual Needs	Lesson Resources
1 **Introduce** *the* **Literature** *Pacing: 1 day*	**Shared Reading and Writing** Warm-up/Build Background, T66 Shared Reading, T66 Shared Writing, T67	**Choices for Rereading,** T67 **Students Acquiring English,** T67	**Poster** I Saw a Purple Cow, T66 *Literacy Activity Book* Personal Response, p. 37
2 **Interact** *with* **Literature** *Pacing: 1–2 days*	**Reading Strategies** Predict/Infer, T68, T72, T78 Summarize, T70, T76 Think About Words, T78 **Minilessons** ✔ Cause and Effect, T69 Feelings, T71 Number Words 1-10, T73 ✔ Written Word as Word, T75 Numbers: Subtracting, T79	**Students Acquiring English,** T78, T80 **Extra Support,** T68, T80 **Challenge,** T69 **Rereading and Responding,** T80-T81	*Literacy Activity Book* Language Patterns, p. 38 **Story Props,** T81 **Audio Tape** for Just for Fun: *Ten in a Bed* See the Houghton Mifflin **Internet** resources for additional activities.
3 **Instruct** *and* **Integrate** *Pacing: 1–2 days*	**Reading/Listening Center** Comprehension, T82 Concept Development, T83 Concepts About Print, T84 Listening, T85 **Independent Reading & Writing,** T86-T87 **Language/Writing Center** Oral Language, T88 Writing, T89 **Cross-Curricular Center** Cross-Curricular Activities, T90-T91	**Challenge,** T88, T89 **Extra Support,** T82, T83, T84 **Students Acquiring English,** T85	*Literacy Activity Book* Comprehension, p. 39 Concept Development, p. 41 Tear-and-Take Story, pp. 43-44 *My Big Dictionary,* T83 **Game** *Monkey Business,* T83, H6 See the Houghton Mifflin **Internet** resources for additional activities.

✔ *Indicates Tested Skills. See page T11 for assessment options.*

1 Introduce *the* Literature

Shared Reading and Writing

Poster

INTERACTIVE LEARNING

Warm-up/Building Background

- Display the poster and explain that the words are from a poem that uses numbers to tell a silly story.

- Invite children to look at the words and listen as you read the poem.

- Have a volunteer explain why the last line is funny. Then read it again, encouraging children to chime in.

- As you reread the poem, have children hold up a finger when you say the number one. When you say two, they should hold up another finger, and so on. At the end of the poem, they should be displaying eight fingers.

- Point out that in this poem, the numbers go from one to eight. Explain that they can also count by starting with the number eight. Tell them that you will read the poem again backwards. This time, every time you say a number, they should put down a finger.

- Help children realize in a general sense that each time they put down a finger, they have one less number.

- Explain that in *Ten in a Bed*, counting the number of children in the bed is an important part of what happens in the story.

Shared Reading

LAB, p. 37

Preview and Predict

- Display the cover of *Ten in a Bed* and read the title and author's name.

- Discuss the cover illustration and invite children to count the number of children in the bed.

- Take a picture walk through the first few pages. Discuss the illustrations pointing out that the children are going to a sleepover at the little one's house.

- Ask children to comment on the expressions on the children's faces and to predict what might happen to the ten children who are all squeezed into one bed.

Read Together   Read the story without interruption. As you read, use your voice to emphasize the number words as well as the words that the little one says. Encourage children to join in as they feel comfortable.

Personal Response   Encourage children to tell what funny things happen in the story when too many children squeeze into the bed. Ask volunteers to tell about the part of the story that they think is the funniest. Then have children complete *Literacy Activity Book* page 37.

Shared Writing: *A Sleep Over*

Brainstorming   Point out that in the story, the children are having a sleepover. Have children imagine what other funny things might happen at a sleepover with ten children. List children's ideas on the chalkboard. Children who have been to a sleepover may want to share their own experiences.

Students Acquiring English Sleepovers may not be common in other cultures. Therefore, it's important to discuss the idea of sleepovers.

Drafting   Have children choose ideas from the list to write a story about some funny things that happen at a sleepover. Have them dictate sentences that you write on chart paper. If children have generated a variety of ideas, you may want to structure them into a cumulative story using number sequence. On chart paper, write: *ONE funny thing that happened at the sleepover was* _____. On the next page, write: *TWO funny things that happened at the sleepover were (add number one) and* _____. Continue until children have included three to five ideas from the list.

Publishing   Have children work with a partner to draw a funny scene for the class story. You might suggest they copy or dictate a sentence about the story onto the bottom of their picture.

Sharing   Share children's drawings and class writing by displaying them on a bulletin board. You may want to place the drawings inside the large frame of a bed and encourage children to provide a title for the class story.

Choices for Rereading

Suggestions for rereading are provided on page T80. These include:

- Listen and Read
- Using the Language Pattern
- Adding a Line
- Listening for Number Words

Literacy Activity Book, p. 37

BIG BOOK

Reading Strategies

▶ **Predict/Infer**

Student Application For the first reading, children predicted what they thought would happen to the ten children in the bed and read with you to find out. In this story, there are many things that happen in the illustrations that aren't in the text. Children can use the illustrations to make inferences about the characters and what other things happen when the children fall out of bed. They might think of questions as you read such as:

- What is the little one like?

- Why do the children go downstairs?

- Where do the children go at the end of the story? How do they feel?

Purpose Setting

Reread the story, pausing periodically to discuss some of the things the children in the illustrations are doing to occupy their time. As you do this, invite children to tell how they think the characters feel or what they might do next.

And the little one said,
"Roll over! Roll over!"
So they all rolled over
And one fell out . . .

8

QuickREFERENCE

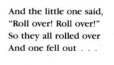

Extra Support

Point out the little one in the illustration as the little girl at the far left side of the bed. Children may not realize that it is the little one's sleepover party. Be sure all children understand that in this story "ten in the bed" means ten children in one bed.

There were TEN in the bed

7

9

Big Book pp. 7, 9

Comprehension
Cause and Effect

TESTED SKILL

Teach/Model

Recall with children the things that happen on pages 7–9. Model for children how they can think about why these things happened.

Think Aloud

The little one says to roll over and a girl gets pushed out of bed. The bed is very crowded, but if the little one hadn't told the others to roll over, the girl probably would not have fallen out of the bed.

Practice/Apply

Have children look at the girl on page 9 and try to figure out how she feels. Ask them what they think has happened to make her feel this way.

SKILL FINDER

Cause and Effect, p. 82

Minilessons, See Themes 8; 11

QuickREFERENCE

MEETING INDIVIDUAL NEEDS
Challenge

Have children look at page 7. How many of the children pictured are awake? (4). Ask them why they think those characters are awake. Encourage creative answers.

2

Interact *with* Literature

Reading Strategies

▶ **Summarizing**

Ask volunteers to summarize the story so far. You might help children by having one volunteer summarize what happens when there are ten in the bed, another volunteer tells what happens when there are nine in the bed, and the third volunteer says what happens when there are eight in the bed. Help children see that summarizing each cumulative verse helps them understand the most important parts of the story and helps them to think about what might happen next.

There were NINE in the bed
And the little one said,
"Roll over! Roll over!"
So they all rolled over
And one fell out . . .

10

There were EIGHT in the bed
And the little one said,
"Roll over! Roll over!"
So they all rolled over
And one fell out . . .

12

Quick**REFERENCE**

Visual Literacy

Help children see that you make your voice a little louder when you read the word NINE because the word is important. Explain that authors sometimes put words in all capital letters so that the reader knows the words are special.

11

13

M I N I L E S S O N

Concept Development

Feelings

Teach/Model

Explain that in this story, children can look at the illustrations to tell a lot about the way the characters feel. Look at pages 10–13 with children and discuss the feelings expressed by the characters, such as:

- (mischievous) the little one
- (surprise) the boy who falls out of bed on page 10
- (shock/surprise) the boy who falls out of bed on page 12

Practice/Apply

- Have children examine the expressions on the faces of other characters on pages 10–13.
- Invite them to find characters who look afraid, angry, mixed up, or amused.
- Ask children to look at the pets on these pages and tell how they are feeling.

SKILL FINDER Minilessons, see Theme 1

Interact *with* Literature

Reading Strategies

▶ **Predict/Infer**

Have children count the children in the illustration on page 14. (6 in the bed and one falling out). Have them predict how many children there are going to be in the bed when they turn the page. (5 with one falling out) Children can infer that since one child falls out of the bed for each verse and set of pages that there will be one less child in the bed and one child falling out when they turn the page.

BIG BOOK

There were SEVEN in the bed
And the little one said,
"Roll over! Roll over!"
So they all rolled over
And one fell out . . .

14

There were SIX in the bed
And the little one said,
"Roll over! Roll over!"
So they all rolled over
And one fell out . . .

16

15

17

Visual Literacy

Have children look at the illustration on page 17. Ask them what the children are doing. Have them make inferences based on the illustration about why the children are going downstairs.

Concept Development

Number Words 1–10

Teach/Model

Point out that in *Ten Black Dots,* children learned about the numbers for 1–10. Write the number 1 on chart paper, and have children read it. Then write the word one next to the number. Explain that this is the word for the number one. In this story all of the numbers are written as words.

Think Aloud

I know that every time I turn the page another child falls out of bed. On p. 14 I know that there were seven in the bed until one fell out. So now I know there are only six in the bed. This word in all capital letters is the word six. It tells me that I can count and find that there are six children in the bed.

Have children count the children in the bed and the one falling out to see that there are six children on the page.

Practice/Apply

- Have children locate the words all in caps for each of the words from one to ten in the story and say them with you.

- If you have the numbers 1–10 displayed in the classroom, add the words for the numbers.

2

Interact
with
Literature

BIG BOOK

There were FIVE in the bed
And the little one said,
"Roll over! Roll over!"
So they all rolled over
And one fell out . . .

18

There were FOUR in the bed
And the little one said,
"Roll over! Roll over!"
So they all rolled over
And one fell out . . .

20

19

21

Big Book pp. 19, 21

 Multicultural Link

Have children look at page 21 and notice what the characters are having for breakfast. (cereal, toast, coffee or tea...) Discuss popular breakfast food in other countries.

 Journal

Have children draw a picture of their favorite character. Invite children to write or dictate a sentence telling why this person is their favorite.

MINILESSON

Concepts About Print

Written Word as Word

TESTED SKILL

Teach/Model

Ask children to close their eyes and listen to how many words you say. Enunciate clearly and slowly as you say: *"Roll over! Roll over!"*

Remind them that we can put a space between words when we talk by saying the words slowly and taking a breath. Explain that when they read words, they will do the same thing. Model how to read written words.

Think Aloud

I see the same words I just said on page 20, *"Roll over! Roll over!"* (Point to each word as you say it.) When I look at them, I see a space between each word. Those spaces separate one word from another. They tell me where to stop for a moment, just like when I say words out loud.

Practice/Apply

Have children track the words in the last two lines on page 20 and read them with you. Ask them to count how many words are in the first line (5) and how many in the second line (4).

SKILL FINDER

Written Word as Word, p. T84

Minilessons, see Theme 4

Ten in a Bed

THEME: JUST FOR FUN

Interact *with* Literature

Reading Strategies

▶ **Summarizing**

Have children look back through the illustrations to help them summarize what the children have been doing since they got out of bed. (brush their teeth, go downstairs, make something to eat, play outside) As you read the end of the story, have children notice how summarizing what has happened in both the words and pictures helps them to understand why the nine children make the little one get up.

There were THREE in the bed
And the little one said,
"Roll over! Roll over!"
So they all rolled over
And one fell out . . .

22

There were TWO in the bed
And the little one said,
"Roll over! Roll over!"
So they all rolled over
And one fell out . . .

24

23

25

Interact *with* Literature

BIG BOOK

There was ONE in the bed
And the little one said,
"I'm not getting up!"
The other NINE said,
"Oh, yes, you are!"

26

28

27

Then there were NONE in the bed
And no one said,
"Roll over! Roll over!"

29

Visual Literacy

Ask children to tell what is happening in the story based on the illustration on page 27. Have them describe what the expressions on the children's faces tell about how they feel — especially the "little one".

Concept Development

Numbers— Subtracting

Teach/Model

Ask children how many children were in the bed in the beginning of the story. (ten) Reread page 26 and ask children how many are left in the bed now. (one) Explain that every time a child fell out of bed, there was one less number of children left in the bed until now there is only one.

Think Aloud

(Hold up ten fingers.) I know that in the beginning of the story there were ten children in the bed, but then one fell out. Let me see, if one child falls out, I need to take away one number. (Put one finger down.) That leaves nine children in the bed — until another one falls out.

Have children use their fingers to continue retelling what happened with you. Each time you say a child falls out of bed, they put a finger down and then tell how many are left. Help them to realize that when they take away one, there is one less number.

Practice/Apply

- Have children take turns using the finger puppet props to count by subtracting one from ten until they have only one puppet left.

SKILL FINDER — Numbers - Subtracting, p. T83

2

Interact with Literature

Rereading

Literacy Activity Book, p. 38

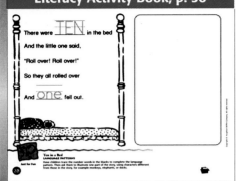

There were __TEN__ in the bed
And the little one said,
"Roll over! Roll over!"
So they all rolled over
And __one__ fell out.

Ten in a Bed
LANGUAGE PATTERNS

Choices for Rereading

Listen and Read

Audio Tape for Just for Fun: *Ten in a Bed*

Extra Support Children can listen to the Audio Tape and follow along in the Little Big Book of *Ten in a Bed* with a partner. Suggest they sit in a make-believe bed in the Reading and Listening Center.

Students Acquiring English This activity enables children acquiring English to hear the natural language patterns.

Listening for Number Words

Use self-stick note to cover the number words in the story. Reread the story and see if children can supply the correct number word that is covered. Give children time to think about the missing word and then uncover the word to see if they are correct.

Adding a Line

For each couple of pages, reread the page with text and then allow volunteers to add a sentence or two telling about the illustration on the facing page. When you reach pages 30–31, children can supply sentences for both illustrations since there is no text on either page.

Language Patterns
LAB, p. 38

Help children identify the repeating verse in the story:

> *There were _____ in the bed*
> *And the little one said,*
> *"Roll over! Roll over!"*
> *So they all rolled over*
> *And one fell out . . .*

Then reread the story and encourage children to clap each time they hear this verse. Finally, have them complete *Literacy Activity Book,* page 38.

Informal Assessment

Choose from the Responding Activities to assess children's general understanding of the story.

Additional Support:
- Reread any confusing sections aloud to help children understand the story.
- Have children use the illustrations to retell the story in their own words.

Responding

Choices for Responding

Count Sheep

Recall with children that the characters in the story fell out of bed one by one and found something else to do when they couldn't sleep. Review the illustrations with children and talk about some of the activities the characters did. Then ask children to tell about things they like to do when they can't sleep.

A Different Verse

Write the first sentence of the story on the board: *There were TEN in the bed and the little one said, "Roll over! Roll over!"* Point out that this is the first sentence of the story and that many of the pages in the story begin with a sentence almost like this one. Then erase the words *roll over* and replace them with another phrase such as *move over* or *wiggle your toes.* Reread the sentence inserting these words. Ask children to add to the list of things the little one might have said.

Finger Puppet Retelling

Provide a table with a cloth draped in front or a puppet theatre for children to re-enact the story using the finger puppets. Children can also make a bed frame out of a large piece of construction paper or oak tag. Children who wish to dramatize the story should practice before presenting the story to the class. You might want to provide a story tape for children to say and follow along with as they use the puppets in their retelling.

Materials
- Finger Puppet Story Retelling Props (See Teacher's Handbook, page H3.)

Portfolio Opportunity

Save *Literacy Activity Book* page 38 as a sample of children's ability to identify language patterns in the story.

Comprehension

Practice Activities

Cause and Effect

LAB, p.39

Extra Support Remind children that in the story, all the children in the bed rolled over and one child fell out. Have them think about why the child fell out. Through demonstration, show children how all the children rolling over caused the one child to fall out of bed.

- Have five children lie down side by side on a blanket or rug. The blanket should cover approximately the same space as the children.

- Read the lines from the story, *"And the little one said, "Roll over! Roll over!" So they all rolled over"* As you say the lines, have children all roll over in a certain direction until one child rolls off the blanket.

- Discuss why one child is no longer on the blanket.

- Children should explain in their own words that all the children rolling over caused the one child to roll off the blanket.

- You might allow a child to lead the reading and continue with the demonstration until only one child is left on the blanket.

- Have children complete *Literacy Activity Book* page 39.

A New Ending

Discuss the idea that a surprise ending helps make a story funnier. Ask children to tell if the story ended the way they thought it would. Then suggest that they think of a funny new ending for the story. Write their suggestions down on chart paper. Encourage pairs of children to choose an idea from the list and act out a funny new ending for the story.

Sounds

Make a recording of several classroom sounds. Play one sound at a time, and have children guess what caused it.
Suggested Sounds:
- pencil sharpening
- paper ripping
- door shutting
- book dropping
- hands clapping

Informal Assessment

As children complete the activities, note whether they can make logical links between causes and effects.

Concept Development

Practice Activities

Numbers: Subtracting

LAB, p. 41

- Give each child ten counters or have children work with a partner.

- Tell children you are going to reread *Ten in a Bed*. As you do, they will remove a counter every time a child in the story falls out of the bed.

- As you read and children remove counters, stop to ask what is happening to the group of counters. Also have them look at the illustrations to note that the number of children in the bed is less and less.

- At the end of the rereading, ask how many counters did they have in the beginning of the story? (ten) How many do they have now? (none) How many counters did they take away from the pile? (ten)

- Have children work with a partner to retell the story on their own removing the counters for each child that falls out of bed.

- Have children complete *Literacy Activity Book* page 41.

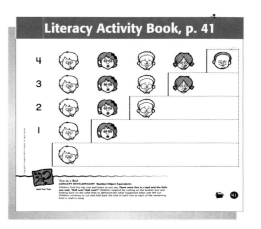

Literacy Activity Book, p. 41

My Big Dictionary

Number Countdown

To give children practice with number subtraction, set up a countdown for something special that is ten days away. As children mark off each day, have them say the number they are crossing off and then how many days are left.

Letter Name Review

Remind children that words are made up of letters and knowing the letters will help them read. Display various alphabet pages in *My Big Dictionary* and invite volunteers to name the capital and small letters.

Extra Support Invite groups of children to play the game *Monkey Business* to practice recognition of capital and lower case letters.

Materials
- Game: *Monkey Business* (See Teacher's Handbook, page H6.)

Portfolio Opportunity

- Save *Literacy Activity Book* page 41 as a sample of children's understanding of numerical identification.

- For a record of how well children understand cause and effect, you might tape-record children's responses to sounds.

Instruct
and
Integrate

Concepts About Print

Practice Activities

Pillow Toss

Have children play in groups of two to four. Make a large game board grid using capital and lowercase letter pairs with which children need practice. Fill two small plastic bags with beans. Cover the bags with cloth and sew or seal with strips of velcro in the shape of small pillows. In turn, each player:

- Tosses one bean bag pillow to any letter on the grid and names the letter.

- Finds the corresponding capital or small letter and tosses a bean pillow to that letter. If a player's bean pillow lands on a matching letter, the player goes again. If a player does not land on a matching letter, the player's turn ends.

- Continues playing until one player has matched three pairs of letters.

Written Word as Word

Extra Support Remind children that when we talk, we pause between words. Similarly, there is a pause between words that are written. Read page 26 of *Ten in a Bed* aloud quickly without taking a breath or pausing between words. Ask children if they could understand what you read. Then have them open to page 26. Read the page again pausing between words. Ask:

- Why was the reading this time different from the first time?

- Have children reread the page with you. Pause at the end of each line and have them count how many words are on the page. Point out that they can see the space between the words on the page and hear the space between the words as they read.

- Continue similarly for the remaining pages.

Informal Assessment

As children complete the listening activities note whether children listen attentively in large groups. Also observe how well children listen for directions and for rhyming words.

Listening

Practice Activities

Listen For Directions

Remind children that whenever the little girl in the story said "Roll over! Roll over!" the other children followed her directions and all rolled over. Invite children to see if they can follow directions like the children in the story. Give simple one-step directions such as the following:

- stand up
- sit down
- clap your hands
- turn around once
- raise your hands

Students Acquiring English This activity allows children to demonstrate comprehension without having to produce the language.

Rhyming Words

Read the repeated verse from the story: "*There were ten in a <u>bed</u> and the little one <u>said</u>,*" emphasizing the rhyming words. Ask children which words have the same ending sounds in the lines you read. (bed/said). Explain that there are many other words that rhyme with *bed* and *said.* Tell them that you are going to say a word. They should stand up if the word rhymes with *bed* and *said.* They should stay seated if the word doesn't rhyme. Include the following words that rhyme with *bed* and *said* along with a variety of unrhymed words: *red, fed, led, sled, sped, shed, Ted.*

Telephone

Ask children what might happen if the little one wanted to get a message to the child at the other end of the bed in a quiet way. Have ten children sit in a row. Tell them that you are going to play a game called "Telephone." You will whisper something to the first child who will pass the message to the second child and so on. They must listen carefully because you can only say the message once. Similarly, they can only whisper the message one time to the child next to them. Say: *Pass the pillow* to the first child. By the end of the line, the message is sure to get scrambled. Play several rounds.

3

Instruct *and* Integrate

Independent Reading & Writing

Surprise!

Surprise!
illustrated by
Susan Meddaugh

This wordless book provides children with an independent book experience that relates to the literature in this theme.

INTERACTIVE LEARNING

Independent Reading
Watch Me Read

Preview and Predict

- Display *Surprise!* Point to the title and illustrator's name as you read them aloud.

- Invite children to describe the things on the cover, including what the characters are doing and where they probably are.

- Take a "picture walk" through the first three pages of the story. Encourage children to discuss the pictures. Help them to realize that there are two things happening in each picture – what the children are doing up front in the picture, and what the other characters are doing in the background.

- Ask children to speculate about the story by discussing what the children in the illustration might have to do with a "surprise." Invite them to predict what the "surprise" will be.

Telling the Story

- Have children use the illustrations to look through the story independently. Suggest that they use the pictures to find out if they were right about the surprise.

- After reading ask:
  What is the big surprise at the end of the story?
  What other surprising things happen in this story?

Rereading

- **Partner Reading** Encourage partners to reread the story cooperatively. Each child can create one or two sentences that tell about each picture. Or they may take turns telling the story to each other.

- **Story Details** Have children reread the story paying attention to the story details that give clues about the surprise party.

Responding

- **Personal Response** Invite children to tell whether they think this was a good surprise and why. Children might also share their own experiences with surprise parties and compare them to the one in the story.

- **Add a Page** Have children draw another page for the wordless story.

Informal Assessment

As children read aloud *Surprise!* and complete other activities, observe their general book-handling skills along with their understanding of the story, as reflected in their oral and written responses.

Student Selected Reading

Library Corner

Place other "fun" books in the Library Corner for children to enjoy. Provide some wordless books that children can use to tell the story to each other.

Favorite Fun Books

Since this theme includes lots of different kinds of books that are "just for fun," invite children to bring in a favorite fun book from home to share with the class. Set aside time each day to read aloud or have children read the books they brought to class.

Student Selected Writing

Just for Laughs

Set up a message board in which children can add and label funny pictures that they find or create.

Fun, How-to-Have

Have children draw and write about ways they have fun. Encourage them to use temporary spelling or dictate their ideas. Display children's ideas on the message board.

Books for Independent Reading

Encourage children to choose their own books. They might choose one of the following titles.

Ten Black Dots
by Donald Crews

Ten in a Bed
by Mary Rees

Have students reread these selections silently or aloud to a partner.

See the Bibliography on pages T6–T7 for more theme-related books for independent reading.

Ideas for Independent Writing

Encourage children to write on self-selected topics. For those who need help getting started, suggest one of the following activities:

- a **sign** for boat do's and don'ts
- an **invitation** to the "little ones" sleep over
- a **counting** book

Portfolio Opportunity

Save examples of the writing children do independently on self-selected topics.

3

Instruct *and* **Integrate**

Oral Language

Choices for Oral Language

Word Web

Create a word web centered around the word *bedtime.* Invite children to name things they associate with bedtime, and print their suggestions on the word web. Read the words with children and invite them to use the words in a sentence.

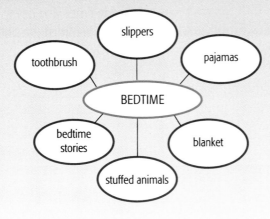

Tear-and-Take Story

LAB, pp. 43-44

Have children remove *Literacy Activity Book* page 43, fold it to make a book, and tell the story to you.

Home Connection Encourage children to take the story home to share it with family members.

Step Right Up

The Little One

Ask children to tell what kind of person they thought the "little one" is. Encourage them to tell if they think she is funny, silly, happy, mean, etc. Ask children if they would like to have the "little one" for their friend and to tell why or why not.

Challenge Have one child act out an emotion (happy, funny, ...) while the others try to guess it. The child who guesses correctly acts out a new emotion for others to guess.

Informal Assessment

Note whether or not children speak in complete sentences. Also observe whether children's writing reflects an understanding of individual words.

 # Writing

Choices for Writing

I'm in the Bed

Present this situation: Suppose you were in the bed in the story. What silly thing would you say or do when the little one said, *"Roll over! Roll over!"*? Ask children to draw a picture of themselves saying or doing something silly. Then invite them to write, or dictate a sentence to tell what they would say or do.

Adapting a Story

 Challenge Children may enjoy making a book based on *Ten in a Bed.* If possible, divide the class into groups of ten. Explain to the groups that they should decide upon a new phrase for the little one to say. They should also decide upon a new location for the children in the story, for example, on a sled, and a new surprise ending for the story.

Have each child choose a different page to illustrate on large construction paper. Then have them write or dictate a verse about their picture using the same pattern as the book. Compile their drawings into a book and have the group work together to make a cover.

Times of Day

Ask children how they react when they hear "It's bedtime" and to tell about the things they like and dislike about this time of day. Similarly, have them tell the things they like and don't like about other times of day: Suppertime; Time for school and Clean-up Time. Then give children a piece of paper that is folded down the middle. As a title for one half, write: *Things I Don't Like About _____.* Title the other half, *Things I Like About _____.* Have children dictate or write a word or words to complete the headings and then draw pictures showing the things they like and don't like about that time of day.

Instruct
and
Integrate

Cross-Curricular Activities

Health

A Good Night's Sleep

Remind children that in the story the children did not have very much sleep at the sleepover. Discuss with children:

- Why sleep is necessary
- What they can try to do if they have trouble going to sleep
- What happens when they don't get enough sleep

You might invite children to create posters which provide tips on how to get the right amount of sleep or how to get to sleep if you are having trouble.

Math

Naming Numbers

Arrange ten chairs in a row. Give each of ten children a number card from one to ten, and invite them to sit in the chairs in numerical order. Invite the remaining children to read the story with you. When the words "Roll over!" are heard, the child holding the number ten card leaves his or her chair and returns to the group. Continue with the rest of the story, having each child leave a chair in turn. Encourage children to do something silly similar to the children pictured in the story as they leave the bed.

Art

Make a Bed

Display page 7 in the Big Book, *Ten in a Bed* and invite children to describe the bed. Then have them talk about other beds they have seen (bunk beds, single beds, pull-out beds and so on). You may want to show children pictures of other types of beds in magazines or advertisements. Then, have children design and decorate beds for their stuffed animals or dolls. Display the finished beds on a table or a shelf in the classroom. Children may want to bring in their stuffed animals or dolls from home to use with the beds.

Materials
- shoe box (each child)
- craft sticks
- colored paper or wallpaper scraps
- fabric scraps
- crayons or markers
- scissors and glue

Drama

What Next?

Display the last spread in the story *Ten in a Bed* and discuss with children what is happening. Ask them to think about where all the children might be going and what they may do now. List their ideas on the chalkboard.

- They are going into the woods to build a fort.
- They are heading off to school.
- They are going to the park to play.

Then invite children to choose a few of the ideas to dramatize.

Theme Assessment Wrap-Up

Reflecting/Self-Assessment

Copy the chart below to distribute to children. Ask them which stories in the theme they liked best. Then discuss what was easy for them and what was more difficult as they read the selections and completed the activities. Have children put a check mark under either *Easy* or *Hard*.

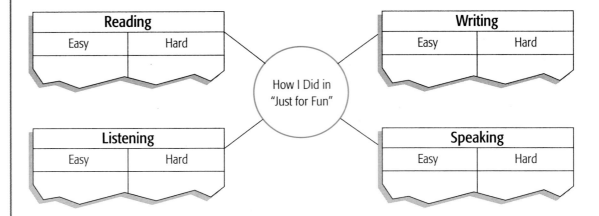

Reading	
Easy	Hard

Writing	
Easy	Hard

How I Did in "Just for Fun"

Listening	
Easy	Hard

Speaking	
Easy	Hard

Monitoring Literacy Development

There will be many opportunities to observe and evaluate children's literacy development. As children participate in literacy activities, note whether each child has a beginning, a developing, or a proficient understanding of reading, writing, and language concepts. The Observation Checklists, which can be used for recording and evaluating this information, appear in the Teacher's Assessment Handbook. They are comprised of the following:

Concepts About Print and Book Handling Behaviors

- Concepts about print
- Book handling

Emergent Reading Behaviors

- Responding to literature
- Storybook rereading
- Decoding strategies

Emergent Writing Behaviors

- Writing
- Stages of Temporary Spelling

Oral Language Behaviors

- Listening attentively
- Listening for information
- Listening to directions
- Listening to books
- Speaking/language development
- Participating in conversations and discussions

Retelling Behaviors

- Retelling a story
- Retelling informational text

Portfolio Opportunity

Invite children to save one piece of work that they did during "Just for Fun".

Choices for Assessment

Informal Assessment

Review the Observation Checklists and observation notes to determine:

- Did children's responses during and after reading indicate comprehension of the selections?
- How well did children understand the skills presented in this theme? Which skills should be reviewed and practiced in the next theme?

Formal Assessment

Select formal tests that meet your classroom needs:

- *Kindergarten Literacy Survey*
- Theme Skills Test for "Just for Fun"

See the *Teacher's Assessment Handbook* for guidelines for administering tests and using answer keys and children's sample papers.

Portfolio Assessment

Evaluating *Literacy Activity Book* Pages

Selected pages from the *Literacy Activity Book* are good to include in children's portfolios as an indication of children's daily work and as a record of their progress in emergent reading and writing.

Saving too many *Literacy Activity Book* pages, however, can quickly create a management problem. These tips can help you keep *Literacy Activity Book* pages under control:

- Plan to save only a few *Literacy Activity Book* pages from each theme. Select pages that show important growth or that reflect areas where a child needs improvement.

- *Literacy Activity Book* pages that include opportunities for writing are useful for evaluating students' emergent writing, temporary spelling, and knowledge of sound/symbol correspondence as well as other targeted skills.

Celebrating the Theme

Choices for Celebrating

Making a Mobile

- Make patterns in the shapes of a boat, a circle, and a bed that children can trace onto the index cards.

- Invite children to decorate the story shapes and make and glue different construction paper people and objects onto the shapes.

- Show them how to cut pieces of yarn and attach them to the shapes. Then attach the other ends of the yarn to the hanger and let the shapes hang to form a theme mobile.

- Cut a piece of construction paper to the shape and size of the triangle formed in the center of the wire hanger. On the paper, write Just for Fun in dotted letters.

- Invite children to trace the letters and hang the triangle in the center of the hanger.

Materials
- assorted construction paper
- wire hanger
- index cards
- crayons, markers
- yarn or string
- scissors and glue

See the Houghton Mifflin **Internet** resources for additional theme-related activities.

A Class Costume Party

If children have been using the "Fun Box" idea, have them celebrate the end of the theme with a costume party. Some preparation ideas:

- Children can plan a parade around the school.

- They can help you post a notice on the school bulletin board or in the school newsletter telling when the parade will take place.

- Children can send an invitation for the parade and party home inviting family and friends to the celebration.

Ten Ways to Say Hurrah!

Make an award board. Invite children to make ten blue ribbons and choose ten of their favorite things about the characters and the stories in this theme.

Write each favorite thing on a blue ribbon and pin it to the award board.

Self-Assessment

Have children meet in small groups to discuss what they learned in the theme. Use the following prompts to spark discussion:

- What was your favorite story? Why was it your favorite?

- Was there a character in one of the stories who you especially like? Who was it? One that you didn't especially like? Who was that?

- Which story, activity, or game was the most fun?

Family Time

Table of Contents
THEME: Family Time

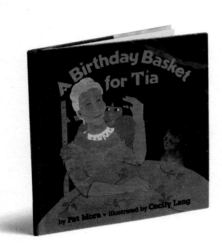

Big Book *LITERATURE FOR WHOLE CLASS AND SMALL GROUP INSTRUCTION*

WATCH ME READ Books *PRACTICE FOR HIGH-FREQUENCY WORDS AND PHONICS SKILLS*

Bibliography

Books for the Library Corner

 Multicultural

 Science/Health

 Math

 Social Studies

 Music

 Art

Picnic
by Emily Arnold McCully
Harper 1984 (32p) also paper
On the way to a picnic, the smallest member of a mouse family gets bounced out of the truck. (wordless)

Nicki's Walk
by Jane Tanner
Modern Curriculum Press 1989
A young boy and his mother take a leisurely walk around his neighborhood. (wordless)

Follow Me!
by Nancy Tafuri
Greenwillow 1990 (24p)
A sea lion pup leaves its napping mother's side to follow a crab. (wordless)

Grandma
by Debbie Bailey
Annick Press 1994 (14p)
Color photographs show children spending time together with their grandmothers.

My Family and Friends
by Lisa-Theresa Lenthall
Rooster 1994 (16p)
Words name different family members and friends.
In English, Spanish, French and German.

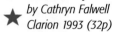

Grandpa
by Debbie Bailey
Annick Press 1994 (14p)
Photographs show children sharing all kinds of different activities with their grandfathers.

Me Too
by Susan Winter
Dorling Kindersley 1993 (24p)
A toddler tries to do everything her older brother does.

Ducks Fly
by Lydia Dabcovich
Dutton 1990 (32p)
His brothers and sisters learn to fly, but one little duck stays behind.

Who's My Baby?
Dorling Kindersley 1994 (12p)
Readers find out which baby animal goes with which mother.

The Ball Bounced
by Nancy Tafuri
Greenwillow 1989 (24p)
A bouncing ball amuses a baby.

We Have a Baby
by Cathryn Falwell
Clarion 1993 (32p)
A new arrival presents opportunities for a big sister to help care for and love the baby.

Books for Teacher Read Aloud

Peter's Chair
by Ezra Jack Keats
Harper 1967 (32p) also paper
Peter gives his outgrown chair to his new baby sister Susie .

A Time for Babies
by Ron Hirshi
Cobblehill 1993 (32)
Photographs present a variety of mammals and birds with their offspring.

Noisy Nora
by Rosemary Wells
Dial 1973 (40p) Scholastic 1993 paper
Nora goes to great lengths to get some attention from the rest of her family. **Available in Spanish as ¡Julieta estate quieta!**

New Shoes for Silvia
by Johanna Hurwitz
Morrow 1993 (32p)
A young girl receives beautiful new red shoes form her Tía Rosita, but finds that they're too big.

Bye-Bye, Baby
by Janet and Allan Ahlberg
LIttle 1990 (32p)
A toddler sets out to find a parent and makes many friends along the way. **Available in Spanish as ¡Adíos, Pequeño!**

Do Like Kyla
by Angela Johnson
Orchard 1990 (32p)
A younger sister's admiration for Kyla leads her to try to do everything Kyla does.

A Baby Just Like Me
by Susan Winter
Dorling Kindersley 1994 (32p)
Martha adjusts to the arrival of her new baby sister.

Koala Lou
by Mem Fox
Harcourt 1988 (32p)
A young koala enters the Bush Olympics to win back her mother's attention.

Poems for Brothers, Poems for Sisters
by Myra Cohn Livingston
Holiday 1991 (32p)
Poems celebrate the relationship between sisters and brothers.

Father Bear Comes Home
by Else Holmelund Minarik
Harper 1959 (64p) also paper
Little Bear welcomes his father home from a fishing trip. **Available in Spanish as Papa Oso vuelve a casa.**

Treasure Nap
by Juanita Havill
Houghton 1992 (32p)
A mother tells her daughter about the cherished possessions her great-grandmother brought to America from Mexico.

Grandmother and I
by Helen E. Buckley
Lothrop 1994 (32p) A child explains why sitting in her grandmother's lap is so special.

Books for Shared Reading

Gone Fishing
by Earlene Long
Houghton 1984 (32p) also paper
A boy and his father spend a companionable day fishing.

Grandmother's Nursery Rhymes/Las Nanas de Abuelita
by Nelly Palacio Jaramillo
Holt 1994 (32p)
A collection of traditional South American riddles, tongue twisters, rhymes, and lullabies. **In English and Spanish.**

Whose Mouse Are You?
by Robert Kraus
Macmillan 1970 (32p) Aladdin 1986 paper
A mouse discovers how much his family loves him. **Available in Spanish as ¿De quien eres, ratoncito?**

Over in the Meadow
by Louise Voce
Candlewick 1994 (32p)
This classic counting rhyme features animal babies and their mothers.

It Wasn't Me
by Alma Flor Ada
Santillana 1992 (14p)
A boy makes a mess as he prepares a special surprise for his mother.
Available in Spanish as No fui yo.

Owl Babies
by Martin Waddel
Candlewick
Three young owls miss their mother.
Available in Spanish as Las lechucitas.

Technology Resources

Computer Software
Internet See the Houghton Mifflin **Internet** resources for additional bibliographic entries and theme-related activities.

Video Cassettes
Noisy Nora *by Rosemary Wells.* Churchill Media
Not So Fast, Songololo *by Niki Daly.* Churchill Media
Picnic *by Emily Arnold McCully.* Churchill Media
I Hate My Brother Harry *by Crescent Dragonwagon.* Churchill Media

Audio Cassettes
Peter's Chair *by Ezra Jack Keats.* HarperAudio
Amanda Pig and Her Big Brother Oliver *by Jean Van Leeuwen.* Listening Library

Filmstrips
Come Away from the Water, Shirley *by John Burningham.* Weston Woods
AV addresses are in the Teacher's Handbook, pp. H15 and H16.

Theme at a Glance

Reading/Listening Center

Selections	Comprehension Skills and Strategies	Phonemic Awareness	Phonics/Decoding	Concepts About Print
A Birthday Basket for Tía	✓ Compare and contrast, T113 Comparing stories, T120 Comparing/contrasting people, T120 Reading strategies, T110, T112, T114, T116 **Rereading and responding,** T118-T119	✓ Recognizing alliteratives, T111 Tongue twisters, T121 Listening for words beginning with same sounds, T121		
Animal Mothers	✓ Topic, details, main idea, T135 Sharing topics and details, T144 Recalling story details, T144 Identifying topics and details in picture books, T144 Reading strategies, T130, T132, T134, T136, T138, T140 **Rereading and responding,** T142-T143		✓ Initial *m*, T131 Supplying words beginning with /m/, T145 Identifying words beginning with /m/, T145 Identify picture names beginning with /m/, T146 Creating /m/ collages, T147	✓ Matching spoken words to print, T133 Matching spoken words to print in a poem, T147 Matching spoken words to print in a story, T147
Me, Too!	✓ Fantasy/realism, T163 Identifying fantasy and realism in stories, T172 Picture clues, T172 Make-believe characters, T172 Reading strategies, T158, T160, T162, T166, T168 **Rereading and responding,** T170-T171		✓ Initial /s/, T161 Decoding *s* words, T173 Spelling *m* and *s* words, T174 Find *s* words, T173 *S* picture book, T173 Initial *s*, T173 Find pictures whose names begin with /s/, T173	✓ Matches spoken words to print, T167 Reading *my* and *said* words, T175 Listening for *my* and *said* words, T175

✓ *Indicates **Tested Skills**. See page T103 for assessment options.*

Families learn from times of giving, caring, and sharing.

This theme is designed to take 2½ to 3 weeks, depending on your students' needs and interests.

This theme can be used in conjunction with themes found in another grade level.
Grade 1: Family Treasures

Language/Writing Center

Cross-Curricular Center

Vocabulary	Listening	Oral Language	Writing	Content Areas
		Making introductions, T122 Telling stories about parties, T122 Naming family members, T122	Writing invitations T123 Writing birthday cards, T123 Writing sand messages, T123 Listing games, T123	**Social Studies:** learning about Mexico, T124 **Music/Creative Movement:** planning a dance party, T125 **Art:** making a piñata, T125 **Science:** supplying words for the five senses, T125
Specific words, T148 Animals and their babies, T148	Learning about animal fathers, T149 Naming animals according to their descriptions, T149 Listening for information about pets and their wild relatives, T149	Telling ways parents keep babies close, T150 Using language patterns, T150 Describing animal parents, T150	Writing animal names, T151 Listing ways to keep babies close, T151 Labeling animal baby illustrations, T151	**Science:** learning about animal families, T152 **Social Studies:** animals around the world, T152 **Math:** sorting animals, T153 **Creative Movement:** animal movements, T153
✓ High-frequency word: *my,* T159 ✓ High-frequency word: *said,* T165 Reading and creating sentences using *my* and *said,* T176 Making books using *my* and *said,* T176 Using *my* and *said* words in sentences, T176 Tear-and-take story, T176	Listening to story, T177 Role-playing an interviewer, T177	Recalling and charting favorite outdoor activities, T180 What family members say, T180 Asking politely to join a group, T180	Designing and decorating greeting cards, T181 Writing about family members, T181 Creating a weather chart, T181 Creating a language experience chart, T181	**Science:** creating a seasonal mural, T182 **Social Studies:** how family members help one another, T182 **Art:** making paper airplanes, T183 **Creative Movement:** balance activities, T183

Meeting Individual Needs

Key to Meeting Individual Needs

 Students Acquiring English

Activities and notes throughout the lesson plans offer strategies to help children understand the selections and lessons.

 Challenge

Challenge activities and notes throughout the lesson plans suggest additional activities to stimulate critical and creative thinking.

 Extra Support

Activities and notes throughout the lesson plans offer additional strategies to help children experience success.

Managing Instruction

Increasing Student Participation

During whole-class instruction use a variety of every-student-response activities to increase the level of participation.

- Think of an idea and share it with a partner.
- If you agree, thumbs up, if you disagree, thumbs down.
- Draw one good idea and hold it up for everyone to see.
- Find something in your book that you want to share with everyone at your table

Every-student responses help satisfy the need for attention and approval from one busy teacher.

For further information on this and other Managing Instruction topics, see the *Professional Development Handbook.*

Performance Standards

During this theme, children will

- *recognize ways that families care and share*
- *make predictions and evaluate them as they read*
- *retell or summarize each selection*
- *apply comprehension skills: Compare and Contrast, Main Idea, Noting Details, Fantasy/Realism*
- *match spoken words to print*
- *recognize alliteratives and words beginning with the sounds for* m *and* s
- *recognize the High-Frequency Words* my *and* said
- *write a story*

Students Acquiring English	Challenge	Extra Support
• **Develop Key Concepts** Children focus on Key Concepts through role-playing and making invitations. • **Expand Vocabulary** Children use context and picture clues, discuss meanings, model and pantomime definitions. Children expand their vocabulary to include family words, names of animals, action words, popular toys, and names for sports. • **Act as a Resource** Children tell about animals from their countries and share their experiences with special holiday foods, birthday treats and songs, and party games from other countries.	• **Apply Critical Thinking** Children apply critical thinking by comparing and contrasting, identifying the topic, main ideas, and details in a selection, and distinguishing between fantasy and realism in a story. • **Explore Across Disciplines** Activities that motivate further exploration include learning about Mexico, exploring animal families, keeping a weather chart, and role-playing. • **Engage in Creative Thinking** Opportunities for creative expression include planning a dance, making piñatas, pantomiming, and creating greeting cards.	• **Enhance Self-Confidence** With extra support provided for reading and responding to the literature, children will see themselves as active members of the reading community. • **Receive Increased Instructional Time on Skill** Practice activities in the Reading/Listening Center provide support with comparing and contrasting, recalling details, and distinguishing between fantasy and reality. • **Provide Independent Reading** Children can take home the Tear-and-Take stories in their *Literacy Activity Books* and the black-and-white versions of the WATCH ME READ titles to read.

Additional Resources

Invitaciones

Develop bi-literacy with this integrated reading/language arts program in Spanish. Provides authentic literature and real-world resources from Spanish-speaking cultures.

Language Support

Translations of Big Books in Chinese, Hmong, Khmer, and Vietnamese. *Teacher's Booklet* provides instructional support in English.

Students Acquiring English Handbook

Guidelines, strategies, and additional instruction for students acquiring English.

Planning for Assessment

Informal Assessment

Observation Checklist

- Concepts About Print/Book Handling
- Responding to Literature and Decoding Behaviors and Strategies
- Writing Behaviors and Stages of Temporary Spelling
- Listening and Speaking Behaviors
- Story Retelling and Rereading

Literacy Activity Book

Recommended pages for students' portfolios:
- Recognizes Alliteratives, p. 49
- Personal Response, p. 50
- Comprehension: Noting Details, p. 52
- Language Patterns, p. 55
- Phonics: Letter *s*, p. 59

Retellings—Oral/Written

- *Teacher's Assessment Handbook*

Formal Assessment

Kindergarten Literacy Survey

Evaluates children's literacy development. Provides holistic indicator of children's ability with
- Shared Reading/ Constructing Meaning
- Concepts About Print
- Book Handling
- Phonemic Awareness
- Letter Recognition
- Emergent Writing

Kindergarten Literacy Survey

Theme Skills Test

- Compare and Contrast
- High-Frequency Words: *my, said*
- Initial *m, s*

Theme Skills Test

Managing Assessment

Work Samples

Question: How can I manage all the work samples I gather to assess my class?

Answer: Try these management tips:

- Don't try to save everything. Determine what areas are most important to assess, and gather materials that show children's progress toward those goals.

- Be flexible. For some children a few samples may be all you need. For others, you may want to gather more information.

- Every month or so, review the work in the portfolio, sending home work that is redundant or no longer needed. Be sure to keep some samples from the beginning, middle, and end of the year so you can document growth over time.

For more information on this and other topics, see the *Teacher's Assessment Handbook*.

Portfolio Assessment

The portfolio icon signals portfolio opportunities throughout the theme.

Additional Portfolio Tips:
- Using Teacher Entry Slips, T185

Launching the Theme

See the Houghton Mifflin **Internet** resources for additional activities.

Song Tape for Family Time: *"Our Family"*

INTERACTIVE LEARNING

Warm-up

Singing the Theme Song

- Play the song "Our Family" for children. See the Teacher's Handbook for lyrics.
- Discuss things in the song that remind children of their own families.
- Play the song again and encourage children to sing along.

Interactive Bulletin Board

Our Families

Peter's family

Marlissa's family

Our Families Invite children to share their families with the class. Children might:

- Draw and label pictures of their families to display on the bulletin board.
- Compare families to see how they are alike and different.
- Bring in photos of family activities to share with classmates.

Lead children to conclude that although families may look different, families members have fun together and love each other.

Ongoing Project

See the *Home/Community Connections Booklet* for theme-related materials.

A Family Get-Together

Invite children to help you organize a Family Get-Together where family members or caregivers can visit to help children celebrate the theme. Children can:

- Plan a simple party with a piñata and the theme song as entertainment.
- Organize party games to play.
- Prepare snacks to serve.
- Decorate the classroom to best display the theme posters and projects.

Portfolio Opportunity

The Portfolio Opportunity icon highlights other portfolio opportunities throughout the theme.

Choices for Centers

Creating Centers

Use these activities to create learning centers in the classroom.

Reading/Listening Center

- Comparing Tía to a Family Member, T120
- "M" Is for Mother Collage, T147
- My Secret Tree House, T174

Language/Writing Center

- Messages in the Sand, T123
- Our Book of Animal Babies, T151
- Me Too! Stories, T181

Cross-Curricular Center

- Art: Make a Piñata T125
- Math: Sorting Animals, T153
- Science: The Four Seasons, T182

READ ALOUD

SELECTION:

A Birthday Basket for Tía

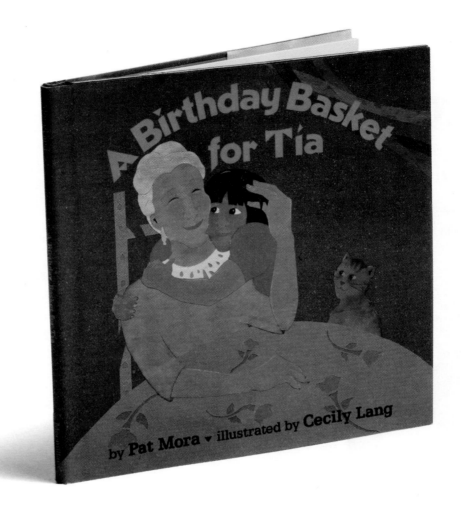

by **Pat Mora** ▾ illustrated by **Cecily Lang**

by Pat Mora

Other Books by the Author

Listen to the Desert

Pablo's Tree

Selection Summary

Cecilia prepares for her beloved great-aunt's ninetieth surprise birthday party. She fills a basket for her Tía with memorabilia from their favorite activities. Tía is deeply touched by Cecilia's birthday basket and the surprise party; then she surprises Cecilia with a dance of celebration and joy.

Lesson Planning Guide

	Skill/Strategy Instruction	Meeting Individual Needs	Lesson Resources
1 **Introduce** *the* **Literature** *Pacing: 1 day*	**Preparing to Listen and Write** Warm-up/Build Background, T108 Read Aloud, T108	Choices for Rereading, T109	**Poster** Others Are Special, T108 *Literacy Activity Book* Personal Response, p. 45
2 **Interact** *with* **Literature** *Pacing: 1–2 days*	**Reading Strategies** Predict/Infer, T110, T114, Evaluate, T110, T112, T114 Summarize, T116 **Minilessons** ✓ Recognizing Alliteratives, T111 ✓ Compare and Contrast, T113	**Extra Support,** T110 **Challenge,** T111 **Students Acquiring English,** T112, T113, T114, T118, T119 **Rereading and Responding,** T118-T119	See the Houghton Mifflin **Internet** resources for additional activities
3 **Instruct** *and* **Integrate** *Pacing: 1–2 days*	**Reading/Listening Center,** Comprehension, T120 Phonemic Awareness, T121 **Language/Writing Center,** Oral Language, T122 Writing, T123 **Cross-Curricular Center,** Cross-Curricular Activities, T124-T125	**Extra Support,** T120, T121 **Challenge,** T121, T123, T124 **Students Acquiring English,** T121, T122	**Posters** Piñata Party, T125 *Literacy Activity Book* Comprehension, pp. 47-48 Phonemic Awareness, p. 49 See the Houghton Mifflin **Internet** resources for additional activities

✓ *Indicates Tested Skills. See page T103 for assessment options.*

1

Introduce *the* Literature

Preparing to Listen and Write

Poster

INTERACTIVE LEARNING

Warm-up/Build Background

Sharing a Poem
- Read aloud "Others Are Special" on the poster.
- Invite children to talk about the poster illustration. Encourage them to think about ways in which they are like these children and ways in which they are different.
- Point out the names of family members, rereading the first three lines of the second verse. Ask how many children have sisters, brothers, aunts, uncles, and grandparents.
- Read the poem again, inviting children to chime in on the names for family members.

Reading Aloud
LAB, p. 45

Preview and Predict
- Display *A Birthday Basket for Tía.* Point to and read aloud the title and the names of the author and illustrator.
- Briefly discuss the cover illustration. Explain that *tía* is the Spanish word for aunt. Have children identify Tía in the picture. Ask how they think the girl, Cecilia, feels about Tía.
- Tell children that in the story, Cecilia helps plan a special birthday party for Tía. Invite children to tell how they celebrate birthdays with their families. Talk about birthday cakes, piñatas, and party games. Then ask if children have ever had a surprise birthday party for a family member. Invite them to share their experiences.
- Read aloud pages 4–9 of the story. Ask children to predict what Cecilia will do with the birthday basket.

Read Aloud
Read the story, pausing occasionally for children to predict what will happen next and to match their predictions to what happens. The following pages are places where you might ask for predictions.
- Page 15: What other things might Cecilia put in the basket?
- Page 23: What will happen at the party?
- Page 27: Will Tía like the birthday basket?

As you read, encourage children to raise their hands when they hear something they don't understand. To help answer their questions, reread the appropriate text and share the accompanying illustrations.

Personal Response

Home Connection Have children complete *Literacy Activity Book* page 45 to show things they would include in a birthday basket for a family member. Invite children to take the page home and retell the story to their families.

More Choices for Rereading Aloud

In addition to the rereading choices suggested here, you may want to use one or more of the activities suggested on page T118.

- Noting Story Patterns
- Listening for the Same Sounds
- Finding Our Favorite Scenes

Choices for Rereading

Telling Chica's Story

Read the story, asking children to listen for sentences that tell about Chica and to look for Chica in the pictures. To promote creative expression, pause after each spread for children to tell how Chica might be feeling and what Chica might say, if she could talk, at this point in the story.

Vocabulary Expansion

As you read, help children recognize the names for family members that are found the story. Ask them to raise their hands when they hear you say *Mamá, Tía, aunt, great-aunt,* and *sisters.*

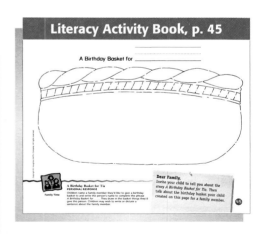

Literacy Activity Book, p. 45

A Birthday Basket for _____

READ ALOUD

Today is secret day. I curl my cat into my arms and say, "Ssshh, Chica. Can you keep our secret, silly cat?"

4

Reading Strategies

▶ **Predict/Infer Evaluate**

Teacher Modeling Remind children that good listeners do many things to help themselves enjoy and understand a story. Good listeners think about the things that happen in a story and try to guess what will happen next. They also ask questions about the things that happen in a story: Does this make sense? Is this what I would do? Model these strategies for children.

Think Aloud

I tried to guess what Cecilia would put in the birthday basket, but I was surprised at some of the things she picked. Then I thought about *why* Cecilia picked each thing. I think Cecilia made some good choices. Each thing she put in the basket reminded her of special times with Tía.

Purpose Setting

Invite children to listen as you read the story again. Say: As you listen to the story this time, think about the reasons why Cecilia put each thing in the basket.

Today is special day. Today is my great-aunt's ninetieth birthday. Ten, twenty, thirty, forty, fifty, sixty, seventy, eighty, ninety. Ninety years old. ¡Noventa años!

At breakfast Mamá asks, "What is today, Cecilia?" I say, "Special day. Birthday day."

6

Mamá is cooking for the surprise party. I smell beans bubbling on the stove. Mamá is cutting fruit—pineapple, watermelon, mangoes. I sit in the backyard and watch Chica chase butterflies. I hear bees bzzzzz.

I draw pictures in the sand with a stick. I draw a picture of my aunt, my *Tía*. I say, "Chica, what will we give Tía?"

7

QuickREFERENCE

Vocabulary

Many Spanish words appear in the story. Their pronunciations are given below the pages in which they first appear: page 4—*Chica* (CHEE cah); page 7—*Tía* (TEE ah); page 6—*noventa años* (noh BEHN tah ah nyohs).

Extra Support

Have children point out the pineapple, watermelon, and mangoes in the pictures on pages 6 and 7. Ask children who have eaten these fruits to tell what they taste like.

Math Link

Ask children to hold up their fingers to show their age. Then ask nine volunteers to come to the front of the room and hold up ten fingers. Tell them that this shows how old Tía is. Help them count the fingers.

Chica and I walk around the front yard and the backyard looking for a good present. We walk around the house. We look in Mamá's room. We look in my closet and drawers.

I say, "Chica, shall we give her my little pots, my piggy bank, my tin fish, my dancing puppet?"

8

I say, "Mamá, can Chica and I use this basket?" Mamá asks, "Why, Cecilia?" "It's a surprise for a surprise party," I answer.

Chica jumps into the basket. "No," I say. "Not for you, silly cat. This is a birthday basket for Tia."

9

I put a book in the basket. When Tia comes to our house, she reads it to me. It's our favorite book. I sit close to her on the sofa. I smell her perfume. Sometimes Chica tries to read with us. She sits on the book. I say, "Silly cat. Books are not for sitting."

10

11

Journal

Have children draw and write about things that Cecilia puts in the birthday basket that remind them of their own family activities.

Challenge

MEETING INDIVIDUAL NEEDS

Ask children to name a word that means the same as close *(near)*. Then ask them to name a word that means the opposite.

Visual Literacy

Pages 10 and 11 mark the beginning of the story's text and picture pattern. The art on the left page shows *what* Cecilia adds to the basket; the art on the right tells *why*. Note that the first thing Cecilia puts in the basket is a book.

Phonemic Awareness

Recognizes Alliteratives

TESTED SKILL

Teach/Model

Have children recall the title of the story: *A Birthday Basket for Tía.*

Think Aloud

When I say this title, I notice that two words begin with the same sound. Listen: *birthday basket.* Do you notice it too? *Birthday* and *basket* begin with the same sound.

Mention that writers sometimes use words that begin with the same sound because they like the way the words sound together.

Practice/Apply

Have children listen as you read pairs of words from the story. Ask them to raise their hand when they hear words that begin with the same sound.

special day	sixty seventy
beans bubbling	dancing puppet
Chica chases	bees buzzzz
good present	secret silly
forty fifty	silly cat

SKILL FINDER

ABC and You Name Game, T121

Minilessons, See Theme 5; 6

Interact *with* Literature

READ ALOUD

I put Tía's favorite mixing bowl on the book in the basket. Tía and I like to make *bizcochos*, sugary cookies for the family. Tía says, "Cecilia, help me stir the cookie dough." She says, "Cecilia, help me roll the cookie dough." When we take the warm cookies from the oven, Tía says, "Cecilia, you are a very good cook."

12 13

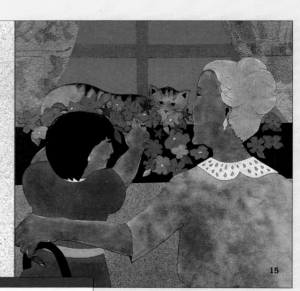

I put a flowerpot in the mixing bowl on the book in the basket. Tía and I like to grow flowers for the kitchen window. Chica likes to put her face in the flowers. "Silly cat," I say.

14 15

Reading Strategies

▶ **Summarize**
Evaluate

Point out that good listeners think as they listen. Help children evaluate Cecilia's choice of items by asking why she put various things in the basket. You might, for example, prompt discussion of the mixing bowl by asking:

- Why does Cecilia put a mixing bowl in the basket?

- Is this a good choice?

- What else could Cecilia put in the basket to remember making cookies with Tía? (Sample answer: rolling pin)

QuickREFERENCE

Vocabulary

The literal translation of *bizcochos* (beez COH chohs), page 12, is "little biscuits." These sugar-topped cookies are part of traditional Christmas celebrations in Mexico.

MEETING INDIVIDUAL NEEDS
Students Acquiring English

To help children understand what Tía and Cecilia did before rolling out the cookie dough, pantomime stirring the dough.

★★★ Multicultural Link

Children of Mexican descent or from Mexico may have enjoyed *bizcochos* during holiday celebrations. Encourage children to tell about special foods that their families share during holidays.

I put a teacup in the flowerpot that is in the mixing bowl on the book in the basket. When I'm sick, my aunt makes me hot mint tea, *hierbabuena.* She brings it to me in bed. She brings me a cookie too.

16

17

I put a red ball in the teacup that is in the flowerpot in the mixing bowl on the book in the basket. On warm days Tía sits outside and throws me the ball.

She says, "Cecilia, when I was a little girl in Mexico, my sisters and I played ball. We all wore long dresses and had long braids."

18

19

MINILESSON

Comprehension

Compare and Contrast

TESTED SKILL

Teach/Model

Explain that thinking about how things are alike and different can help children to better enjoy and understand a story. Ask children to think about ways in which Cecilia and Tía are alike and different.

Think Aloud

Cecilia and Tía like doing many of the same things, like making cookies. But the words and pictures in the story also tell me how they are different. One way that Cecilia and Tía are different is that Cecilia is a young girl and that Tía is an old woman.

Practice/Apply

Have children draw pictures to show one way in which Cecilia and Tía are alike and one way in which they are different. Ask children to share their drawings with the class and tell about the similarities and differences.

SKILL FINDER

Comparing Stories p. T120

Minilessons, See Themes 8;12

Students Acquiring English

MEETING INDIVIDUAL NEEDS

On page 16, Tía's hot mint tea, *hierbabuena,* is pronounced (yeer bah BWAY nah). Invite any Spanish speakers to talk about the tea.

Health/Nutrition Link

Talk about things people do and drink or eat when they are sick to help them feel better, for example, take cool baths or eat hot soup.

Social Studies Link

On page 18, we learn that Tía grew up in Mexico. Help children locate Mexico on a map of North America. Talk about where they live in relation to Mexico.

2

Interact
with
Literature

Reading Strategies

▶ **Predict/Infer
Evaluate**

Remind children that they can use word and picture clues to help them figure out things that will happen in a story.

Display pages 26 and 27 and reread them. Talk about how the words and pictures help show what Tía's party is like. Note details that show how noisy and festive the party is: the guests shouting their greetings, the musicians playing their instruments, and Cecilia and Tía laughing. Then ask children which things on these pages that help them figure out that Tía might have a good time at her surprise party. (There's music and she might like singing and dancing; everyone shouts Happy Birthday; she laughs.)

Encourage children to talk about how this party looks like more or less fun than the parties they have attended.

Students Acquiring English
These strategies encourage children to use different cues and to draw on their own background knowledge.

READ ALOUD

Chica and I go outside. I pick flowers to decorate Tía's basket. On summer days when I am swinging high up to the sky, Tía collects flowers for my room.

20

Mamá calls, "Cecilia, where are you?"

Chica and I run and hide our surprise.

I say, "Mamá can you find the birthday basket for Tía?"

Mamá looks under the table. She looks in the refrigerator. She looks under my bed. She asks, "Chica, where is the birthday basket?"

Chica rubs against my closet door. Mamá and I laugh. I show her my surprise.

After my nap, Mamá and I fill a piñata with candy. We fill the living room with balloons. I hum, mmmmm, a little work song like the one Tía hums when she sets the table or makes my bed. I help Mamá set the table with flowers and tiny cakes.

22

23

Vocabulary

Point out the *piñata* (peen YAH tah). Explain that to play the piñata game guests are blindfolded, turned around a few times, and given a chance to break the *piñata* with a stick. When it breaks, guests race to gather the treats.

 Multicultural Link

Note that many party games come from other countries. You might share the Israeli *Without Hands*. (Team players stand along a row of hats and hold a rope. They race to put on the hats using anything but their hands!)

 Multicultural Link

Point out the tiny cakes for Tía's party. Invite children to name other special birthday foods. In Russia, people eat birthday pies; in Iceland they eat thin pancakes sprinkled with sugar and rolled up with fruit and whipped cream.

"Here come the musicians," says Mamá. I open the front door. Our family and friends begin to arrive too.

I curl Chica into my arms. Then Mamá says, "Sshh, here comes Tía."

I rush to open the front door. "Tía! Tía!" I shout. She hugs me and says, "Cecilia, *¿qué pasa?* What is this?"

24

"SURPRISE!" we all shout. "*¡Feliz cumpleaños!* Happy birthday!" The musicians begin to play their guitars and violins.

"Tía! Tía!" I say. "It's special day, birthday day! It's your ninetieth birthday surprise party!" Tía and I laugh.

26

27

Vocabulary

Encourage children to say *¿qué pasa?* (KAY PAH sah), *What is this?* and to shout *¡feliz cumpleaños!* (feh LEEZ cuhm pleh AH nyos), *Happy Birthday!* like Cecilia and the guests.

Phonemic Awareness Review

Read the first two sentences on page 27, asking children to listen for rhyming words. Have them suggest other words that rhyme with *say* and *day.*

A Birthday Basket for Tía

Interact *with* Literature

READ ALOUD

Reading Strategies

▶ Summarize

Display the following pages and model for children how to summarize the story:

Think Aloud

- Pages 8–9: I look at some pages at the beginning of the story and I remember that Cecilia wants to find a good present for Tía.

- Pages 10–12: Now I look at some pages in the middle of the story and I remember that Cecilia fills a birthday basket with things that remind her of things she and Tía like to do together.

- Pages 28–32: Last, I look at some pages at the end of the story and I remember that Cecilia surprises Tía with the birthday basket; Tía surprises Cecilia by dancing with her.

Self-Assessment

Encourage children to think about their reading by asking themselves these questions:
• Have I been asking myself questions and looking for the answer?
• What did I do if I didn't understand something?
• Have I been thinking about what I like or don't like about a story.

Chica. Everyone laughs.

Then the music starts and my aunt surprises me. She takes my hands in hers. Without her cane, she starts to dance with me.

32

2

Interact with Literature

Rereading

More Choices for Rereading

Noting Story Patterns

As you read, help children note the cumulative story line by having them complete sentences that name the items in the basket, for example: *I put a (book) in the* (basket). If needed, point to the item in the illustration that completes the sentences. Or, display the sentences on chart paper and ask children to help you read them as you reach that part of the story.

Students Acquiring English This activity shows children how they can use syntax and picture clues as they read.

Finding Our Favorite Scenes

Invite children to relate the story to their feelings by having them stand when you read about activities Cecilia and Tía do together that they would also like to do. Ask those standing to tell why they especially liked these parts.

Listening for the Same Sounds

To help children recognize alliterative phrases, read the story pausing now and then to reread word pairs that begin with the same sound *(bowl, book)* and those that don't *(cookie, dough)*. Ask children if the words begin with the same sounds.

Informal Assessment

Use the Story Talk, Tía's Birthday Basket, or the retelling activity to assess children's general understanding of the selection.

Additional Support:

- Reread any confusing sections aloud.
- Take children on a "picture walk" through the story and summarize what is happening as you turn the pages.

Responding

Choices for Responding

Story Talk

Place children in groups of two or three, and have them respond to one or more of the following:

- Who is the oldest person in your family? How is this person like Tía? How is he or she different?

- Tell about a birthday surprise you might plan for a family member. What special foods would you make? How would you decorate your house?

Students Acquiring English If some students have very limited language proficiency, they could talk about these topics in their primary languages in same–language groups.

Retelling *A Birthday Basket for Tía*

Materials
- Story Retelling Props–Teacher's Handbook, H4

Help children to use the templates to make the Story Retelling Props for *A Birthday Basket for Tía.* Invite them to retell the story using the props. Encourage them to role-play Cecilia as they choose items to place in the basket and tell why the items are important.

Students Acquiring English Let children combine language with pantomime to show how various items were used in the activities Cecilia and Tía enjoy together.

Special Memories Show-and-Tell

Invite children to bring in from home items that remind them of special times spent with family members. Children can take turns displaying their items and telling about them. Encourage listeners to ask questions about the items and the special memories that go with them.

Tía's Birthday Basket

Have children draw pictures of how Tía's birthday basket looked after it was filled. Encourage children to write, or dictate, a sentence about their pictures and to use them to retell the story to partners.

Portfolio Opportunity

For a writing sample, save children's drawings from Tía's Birthday Basket.

Instruct
and
Integrate

Comprehension

Literacy Activity Book, p. 47

Cecilia	Cecilia and Tía	Tía

Practice Activities

Comparing Stories

MEETING INDIVIDUAL NEEDS

Extra Support Remind children that thinking about ways things are alike and different can help them understand these things better. Display *Mr. Rabbit and the Lovely Present,* and ask children to tell what they remember about the story. Read the story aloud, asking children to listen for ways it is like *A Birthday Basket for Tía* and ways it is different.

- Both the little girl and Cecilia want to find something. What do they want to find? (good birthday presents) Think about who the presents are for. How is this different? (The little girl wants a gift for her mother; Cecilia wants a gift for her great-aunt, Tía.)

- Both girls choose things, but they choose in different ways. How is the way they choose different? (The little girl chooses things with colors her mother likes; Cecilia chooses things that show activities she and Tía do together.)

- Both stories tell about birthday baskets, but one story is make-believe and one is not. Which story is make-believe? (Mr. Rabbit and the Lovely Present) Which story could really happen? (A Birthday Basket for Tía)

Alike and Different

LAB, p. 47

Review with children ways in which Cecilia and Tía are alike and ways in which they are different. Page through the story, with children, helping them to use word and picture clues to compare and contrast Cecilia and Tía's actions, their appearance, and Tía's actions before and after she receives Cecilia's birthday basket.

Then have children complete *Literacy Activity Book* page 47 to show ways in which Cecilia and Tía are alike and different.

Comparing Tía to a Family Member

Ask children to think of a family member or friend who is like Tía. Suggest they draw pictures to show one way that the person they chose is like Tía and one way that person is different. Encourage children to write, or dictate, sentences about their drawings. Have small groups share and discuss their work.

Informal Assessment

As children complete the activities, note whether they are able to compare and contrast items. Also observe whether children can distinguish and produce words that have the same beginning sound.

Phonemic Awareness

Practice Activities

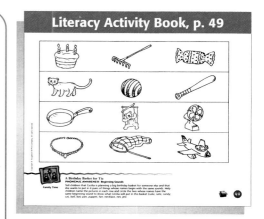

ABC and You Name Game

LAB, p. 49

Display the Big Book *ABC and You.* Recall the alphabet book with children. Invite small groups of children to take turns listening to the *ABC and You* Audio Tape. Have them listen for words and names that begin with the same sounds.

Challenge Have children find the page in *ABC and You* that corresponds to their own names. Invite them to create similar pages for their names, using the given adjectives or supplying new ones that begin with the same sounds.

Have children complete *Literacy Activity Book* page 49 to practice recognizing picture names that begin with the same sound.

Alliterative Nursery Rhyme Names

Extra Support Remind children that some words in the story, like *birthday basket* and *Chica chases,* began with the same sounds. Invite children to listen as you say nursery rhyme names. Have them raise their hands when they hear names that begin with the same sounds and repeat them after you.

If children in your class have alliterative names, extend the activity by reciting them, along with a few others, for children to listen to and name as beginning with the same sounds.

Tongue Twisters

Have children explore alliteratives by reciting tongue twisters.

> Rubber baby buggy bumpers
>
> Peter piper picked a peck of pickled peppers;
> A peck of pickled peppers Peter Piper picked.
> If Peter piper picked a peck of pickled peppers,
> Where's the peck of pickled peppers Peter Piper picked?

Students Acquiring English Invite children to first work with family members and then say a tongue twister in their primary language for other students to hear and attempt to repeat.

Portfolio Opportunity

For a record of children's understanding, of alliteratives save *Literacy Activity Book* page 49. Also keep children's work comparing Tía with a family member.

3

Instruct *and* Integrate

Oral Language

Choices for Oral Language

Names For Family Members

Remind children that Cecilia made the birthday basket surprise for her aunt, Tía. Invite children to think of other words, like *aunt,* that name family members. Chart children's responses, if different names for the same family member are suggested, include them.

Students Acquiring English Invite children to share names for family members in other languages. Have all children compare and contrast these names to their English equivalents. For example, children may note that *Mother* and the Spanish *Mamá* begin with the same sounds while *Aunt* and *Tía* do not.

Making Introductions

Recall the many friends and family members who came to Tía's party. Point out that at big parties, there may be people who don't know one another. Ask two children to come to the front of the room. Demonstrate how to introduce them. Children can then form groups of three to practice introducing one another.

Party Time

Have children recall how Cecilia and her mother got ready for Tía's party. Then invite children to tell about parties they've helped their families get ready for. Suggest they draw pictures and use them in their talks. Children's talks should address the following:

- Who the party was for
- How they helped get ready for the party
- What foods they served
- What games they played

Informal Assessment

As you complete the activities, note whether children speak clearly and use appropriate volume. Also observe whether children offer initial consonants or invented spellings of unknown words.

 # Writing

Choices for Writing

Invitations to a Birthday Party

Display several birthday invitations for children to examine. Note the special places to write the name, date, time, and place of the party. Then help children to fill out a birthday invitation together. Provide children with additional birthday invitation forms to complete on their own. Children can fill out the invitations for Tía's party or a party they'd like to have. Invite children to decorate the invitations any way they wish.

Birthday Cards for Tía

Materials
- drawing or construction paper
- markers or crayons

Have children make birthday cards for Tía. Show them how to fold a sheet of drawing paper in half to make a "card." Ask them to write *Happy Birthday* on the outside of the card and suggest that they decorate the inside of the card with things they'd like to give to Tía.

Messages in the Sand

Materials
- bag of sand
- small scoop (for sprinkling sand onto tray)
- shallow tray or cookie sheet with low sides

Remind children that Cecilia drew pictures in the sand as she tried to think of a present for Tía. Sprinkle enough sand into the tray so that children can write or draw in it with an object or their fingers. Invite them to draw or write in the sand and discuss why it is such fun.

Challenge Invite children to write in the sand all of the letters of the alphabet.

Party Games

Remind children that Cecilia and Mamá fill a piñata with candy so everyone can play the piñata game at Tía's party. Ask them to name other party games. List the games suggested on chart paper, asking children to help you spell words for which they know the initial consonant sounds. Then invite them to choose one of the games to play.

Portfolio Opportunity

Save children's birthday cards as a sample of their ability to copy or write letters.

Cross-Curricular Activities

Social Studies

A Visit to Mexico

Challenge Mention that Tía grew up in Mexico, and help children find Mexico on a map of North America. Ask what children know about Mexico, making sure they understand that Spanish is spoken. Invite children to look at the books to learn more about Mexico. If children have family members from Mexico or of Mexican descent, invite them to speak with the class.

Materials
- map of North America
- picture books on Mexico

Music

Dance Party

Talk about how Tía surprised Cecilia by dancing, without her cane. Then suggest that children plan their own dance party. Invite them to bring in their favorite party music from home, and bring in some of your own as well. Begin the dance party by teaching children dances such as "The Bunny Hop," "The Hora," and the "The Hokey-Pokey" to help them abandon any shyness. Move on to the music children brought in for free-form dance. Encourage children to talk about the songs and dances they liked best.

Materials
- recordings of participatory dance music such as "The Bunny Hop," "The Hora," or "The Hokey-Pokey"
- cassette player

Art

Make a Piñata

Display the poster and discuss it with children. Ask children to identify the materials needed and help them review the steps to follow.
Invite children to help you make a piñata, or have them work in
groups to make several piñatas. They can save the piñata(s) for the
Family-Get-Together or for their own theme celebration. Depending on the
abilities of your children, you may wish to ask for parent volunteers to
come in for an hour or two over the course of a week to supervise group
work and assist children.

Materials
- Piñata Party
  poster
- materials listed on
  the poster

Science

My Five Senses

Mention to children that there were lots of things Cecilia could see, hear,
smell, taste, and touch in the story. Invite children to help you make a chart
of the five senses to talk about some of these things. As children suggest
items for the chart, prompt them to supply words that tell how the things
look, sound, smell, taste, and feel.

BIG BOOK

SELECTION:
Animal Mothers

Big Book

Little Big Book

● **Best Books for Children**

by Atsushi Komori

Other Books by the Author

Animals Sleeping

Selection Summary

With simple language and realistically rendered pictures, children are introduced to various animal mothers and the ways in which they keep their babies close.

Lesson Planning Guide

	Skill/Strategy Instruction	Meeting Individual Needs	Lesson Resources
1 Introduce *the* Literature *Pacing: 1 day*	**Shared Reading and Writing** Warm-up/Build Background, T128 Shared Reading, T128 Shared Writing, T129	**Choices for Rereading**, T129 **Students Acquiring English**, T129	**Poster** Travel Plans, T128 *Literacy Activity Book* Personal Response, p. 50
2 Interact *with* Literature *Pacing: 1–2 days*	**Reading Strategies** Predict/Infer, T130 Self-Question, T130, T134 Monitor, T130, T134 Evaluate, T132, T140 Summarize, T136, T140 Think About Words, T138 **Minilessons** ✔ Initial *m*, T131 ✔ Matches Spoken Words to Print, T133 ✔ Topic, Details, Main Idea, T135	**Extra Support,** T132, T136, T138 **Challenge**, T139 **Rereading and Responding**, T142-T143 **Students Acquiring English**, T130, T133, T142, T143	*Literacy Activity Book* Language Patterns, p. 51 **Picture, Letter, and Word Cards,** T131 **Audio Tape** for Family Time: *Animal Mothers,* T142 See the Houghton Mifflin **Internet** resources for additional activities
3 Instruct *and* Integrate *Pacing: 1–2 days*	**Reading/Listening Center,** Comprehension, T144 Phonics/Decoding, T145-T146 Concepts About Print, T147 Vocabulary, T148 Listening, T149 **Language/Writing Center,** Oral Language, T150 Writing, T151 **Cross-Curricular Center,** Cross-Curricular Activities, T152-T153	**Extra Support,** T144, T145, T146, T147 **Students Acquiring English,** T144, T148, T151, T153 **Challenge,** T148, T152	**Poster** Animal Parents, T150 *Literacy Activity Book* Comprehension, p. 52 Phonics/Decoding, p. 53 **Picture, Letter, and Word Cards,** T145, T146 **My Big Dictionary,** T146 **Game:** *Busy Families,* T145, H8 **Audio Tape** for Family Time: *Animal Mothers,* T147, T149 See the Houghton Mifflin **Internet** resources for additional activities

✔ *Indicates Tested Skills. See page T103 for assessment options.*

Introduce *the* **Literature**

Shared Reading and Writing

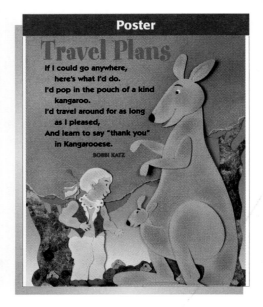

Poster

Travel Plans

If I could go anywhere,
here's what I'd do.
I'd pop in the pouch of a kind
kangaroo.
I'd travel around for as long
as I pleased,
And learn to say "thank you"
in Kangarooese.

BOBBI KATZ

INTERACTIVE LEARNING

Warm-up/Build Background

Sharing a Poem
- Read aloud "Travel Plans" on the poster.

- Invite children to share what they know about kangaroos. Ask if they think it would be fun to ride around in a kangaroo's pouch.

- Note that the kangaroo and her baby are a family. Invite children to talk about other animal families they've seen. Prompt discussion by asking:

  Have you seen a mother cat with her kittens? How does a mother cat care for her family?

  Have you seen a nest of baby birds? How does a mother and father bird care for its family?

  What movies or television shows have you seen about animal families? How did the mother or father animal care for their babies?

Shared Reading

LAB, p. 50

Preview and Predict
- Display *Animal Mothers*. Point to and read aloud the title and the names of the author and illustrator. Briefly discuss the cover, asking children to tell what the mother fox is doing.

- Display and read aloud pages 4 and 5 of the story. Have children identify the mother cat and her kittens. Help them use the text and picture details to predict what the selection will be about.

- Take a picture walk through page 11, noting that the selection tells about real animals and how they act. Invite children to predict what other animals they might read about.

Read Together
- Read the selection aloud, encouraging children to join in with words they know. Point to the words using a sweeping left to right motion.
- As you read, invite children to comment on the illustrations.

Personal Response

Have children complete *Literacy Activity Book* page 50 to show which of the animal mothers and babies they liked the best.

Shared Writing: *A Class Story*

Brainstorming

Remind children that the Big Book *Animal Mothers* told about animal mothers and their babies. Invite children to write their own story about animal families. Brainstorm with them a list of topics they might write about. Help children create a web for the one they choose.

Drafting

Have children contribute sentences to the class story. Record their suggestions on chart paper. Model keeping to the topic as needed.

Think Aloud

Yes, mother tigers also hunt for food. But our story is about lion families. Let's see if we can think of another sentence to tell about lion families.

Students Acquiring English Drafting together enables children to contribute more or less, depending on their proficiency level. Even if students acquiring English cannot contribute directly, they can follow the activity.

Publishing

Copy the sentences onto drawing paper and ask volunteers to make illustrations to go with them. Bind the pages into a class book for the Reading and Listening Center.

Choices for Rereading

Rereadings enable children to focus on different aspects of a story and to respond to it in varying ways. You may want to use some or all of the rereading choices on page T142.

- Listen and Read!
- Recognizing Language Patterns
- Pantomime the Story
- Listening for Initial *m*

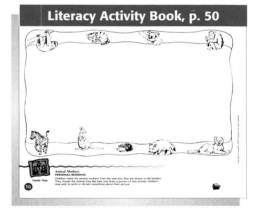

Literacy Activity Book, p. 50

Portfolio Opportunity

Save *Literacy Activity Book* page 50 as a sample of children's personal response to the story.

2

Interact *with* Literature

Reading Strategies

▶ **Predict/Infer**
  Self-Question
  Monitor

Discussion Remind children of the things good readers and listeners do to help them understand and remember a story: they make predictions about the things they will learn in a story; they think about what they hear and read.

Review the predictions children made before reading this story. Ask what questions they had while reading the story and record them for later use. *(Why does the animal mother act this way? What other animals act this way?)*

Purpose Setting

Invite children to read the story to see if their questions are answered. Help them use words and picture clues to answer their questions.

BIG BOOK

Mother cat carries her kittens in her soft mouth.

4

Mother lion carries her cub in her mouth, too.

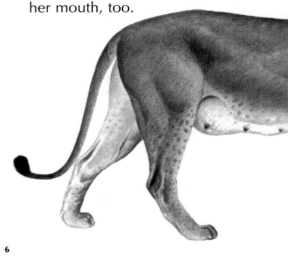

6

Math Link

Have children count the number of kittens they see on page 5. Talk about how many kittens the mother cat can carry at one time. Ask how this might cause problems for the mother cat.

 Students Acquiring English

Word Meaning Point out to children the different names for baby cats (*kittens*) and baby lions (*cubs*). Ask children to point to each one in the illustrations.

5

7

Media Link

Ask if children have seen television shows or movies about lions. Invite those who have to tell how they compare to the picture in the story. What other things did they learn about lion families from the television program or movie?

Science Link

Tell children that house cats and lions are alike in many ways. Invite them to look at the pictures and tell how they are alike.

M I N I L E S S O N

Phonics/Decoding

Initial *m*

Teach/Model

Read aloud the sentence on page 4, pointing to the words as you say them. Frame *mother* and have children name the first letter. *(m)* Ask children to say *mother,* listening for the beginning sound. Conclude that *m* stands for the sound at the beginning of *mother.*

Display Magic Picture *monster.* Explain that Magic Picture *monster* can help children remember the sound for *m.* Have children say *mother* and *monster,* listening for the beginning sounds. Then ask them to pretend that they are monsters thinking of something good to eat. Have children rub their stomachs and make the /*m*/sound.

Practice/Apply

Read page 6. Then read it again, pausing for children to read the word *mother.* Then reread the sentence, asking children to say "Mmm" when they hear a word that begins like *mother* and *monster.* Frame the word *mouth* and have a volunteer point to the initial *m.* Have children say *mother* and *mouth,* listening for the beginning sounds.

SKILL FINDER Picture Card Activity, p. T145

Interact
with
Literature

Reading Strategies

► **Evaluate**

Remind children that good readers and listeners think about what they hear and read. Encourage children to compare the way the book shows a baboon mother carrying its baby to the way it shows a chimpanzee carrying its baby. Ask children if the ways make sense to them and why.

BIG BOOK

Mother baboon's baby clings tightly to her stomach.

8

Mother chimpanzee carries her baby in her arms.

10

QuickREFERENCE

Journal

Ask children to keep track of the animals in the selection by drawing pictures or writing down the animals' names in their journals.

MEETING INDIVIDUAL NEEDS
Extra Support

Tell children that *clings* means holds tightly. Show how you might hold someone's hand versus how you might cling to it to illustrate the difference between *holding* and *clinging*.

9

Concepts About Print

Matches Spoken Words to Print

Teach/Model

TESTED SKILL

Display page 8. Tell children that you will read the first word on this page. Read *Mother,* and call on a volunteer to point to the word. Then guide children in realizing how to recognize a word.

Think Aloud

We put letters together to make words. Each group of letters on this page is a different word. The first word on this page is *Mother.* The next group of letters is another word; the word is *baboon's.* The next group of letters is the word *baby.* (Follow this procedure with the rest of the sentence.)

Note the space that separates each group of letters. Then invite children to help you count the words on the page.

Practice/Apply

Repeat the procedure with other pages from the story. As you read each page, word for word, have volunteers point to the group of letters that make up the word. Count the number of words found on the pages with children.

SKILL FINDER Reading a Poem, p. T147

Science Link

Tell children to tell how the baboon and the chimpanzee are different. Explain that a baboon is a kind of monkey, having a tail and walking on all four legs. The chimpanzee is a kind of ape. Apes do not have tails and they walk on two legs.

MEETING INDIVIDUAL NEEDS
Students Acquiring English

Have children who know the names of some animals in other languages say them for the class.

Technology Link

Invite children to view and listen to wild animals on a CD-ROM encyclopedia or take a multimedia tour of the San Diego Zoo to visit these creatures in *The Animals!* (MPC/MAC).

Big Book pp. 9, 11

Animal Mothers **T133**

Interact *with* Literature

Reading Strategies

▶ **Self-Question Monitor**

Remind children that good readers and listeners stop while reading to make sure they understand what is happening in a story. Ask if any of their questions about the story have been answered. Encourage them to tell how they use the words and pictures to answer their questions.

You might, for example, talk about pages 12–15: Did children wonder why the koala cub clings to its mother's back, while the sloth baby clings to its mother's stomach? Do the pictures on these and other pages in the story help them to begin to answer their questions?

BIG BOOK

12

14

Quick**REFERENCE**

Background: ᶠʏI

Koalas are marsupials; they carry their cubs in a pouch for six months until they mature and are old enough to be carried on their mother's backs.

Science Link

Ask children to name the animal parts of the body they've read about so far (mouth, stomach, arms, back). Have children identify these parts of the body on the story animals and then on themselves.

Mother koala's cub
rides on her back.

13

Mother sloth carries her
baby on her stomach.

Comprehension

Topic, Details, Main Idea

Teach/Model

Tell children that they can often tell in just a few words what a story is mostly about. Ask what this story is mostly about. (animal mothers)

Then talk with children about the main idea the author wants us to learn about these animal mothers: they have different ways of keeping their babies close. Ask why children think animal mothers want to keep their babies close. (to watch over them and keep them safe, to carry them, to feed them, to clean them, to teach them)

Tell children that clues in the words and pictures tell how each animal mother keeps her baby close. Display pages 14 and 15, and read the sentence. Help children find word and picture details that tell how a mother sloth keeps its baby close.

Practice/Apply

Ask volunteers to note details in other pictures that show the different ways that animal mothers keep their babies close.

SKILL FINDER

Topic and Details, p. T144

Minilessons, See Themes 10, 11

Background: FYI

Sloth are slow-moving, leaf-eating animals that live in the rain forests of Central and South America. They spend most of their lives upside down in trees.

Science Link

Mention to children that many animals live in trees. Ask children to look at the pictures of the animals in this story. Which ones live in trees? How can they tell?

2

Interact
with
Literature

BIG BOOK

Mother kangaroo carries her joey in her pouch.

16

18

Reading Strategies

▶ **Summarize**

Recall that good readers and listeners think about the most important things in a story to help them understand and remember it. Ask children what the story was about. (animal mothers) Then ask them what it told them about animal mothers. (how they keep their babies close) Then guide children through the book to page 19 and invite them to comment on how each animal mother does that.

QuickREFERENCE

Extra Support

Some children may be unfamiliar with the names of various animal features such as the kangaroo's *pouch,* or the elephant's *trunk* on pages 16–19. Help children identify these features from the pictures.

Background: FYI

As with most marsupials, female kangaroos give birth to tiny young who continue to develop in their mother's pouch. A joey spends between six to eight months in its mother's pouch before venturing out on its own.

17

Mother elephant gently pushes her baby with her trunk to make it run.

19

Interact
with
Literature

Reading Strategies

▶ **Think About Words**

Display page 20 and discuss how children can figure out *mother*.

The story says: *The zebra foal runs along behind its _____.*

- **What makes sense** We've been reading about animal mothers and how they keep their babies close.

- **Sounds for letters** Point to the word *mother,* noting that it begins with the letter *m.*

- **Picture clues** The picture shows a zebra foal running along behind a large zebra. That large zebra is the mother.

Have children reread the sentence with you to see if *mother* makes sense.

The zebra foal runs along behind its mother.

Baby wild boars follow their mother all in a bunch.

22

QuickREFERENCE

Science Link

Help children make comparisons between the zebra and the horse. Point out that both zebras and horses have foals. Ask children other ways the animals are alike and different.

Extra Support

Ask children what they think *foal* means. (baby zebra) Help them use the story pattern and the pictures to figure out the word meaning.

21

23

Challenge

Some children may enjoy listing the special names for animal babies mentioned in the story. Encourage these children to keep their lists for use in a later activity.

Science Link

Ask children if they can name an animal that looks like the mother wild boar. (pig) Show children a picture of a pig and then invite them to compare wild boars to pigs.

Interact *with* Literature

Reading Strategies

▶ **Evaluate**

Invite children to share their feelings about the story. Prompt discussion by asking:

- Do you like this story? Why?
- What new things did you learn?
- Do you think all the things you learned are true? Why or why not?

▶ **Summarize**

Discuss how good readers and listeners think about the most important parts of a story to help them remember it. Ask children to think about the most important parts of this story and tell about them.

Baby hedgehogs follow their mother in a nice straight line.

24

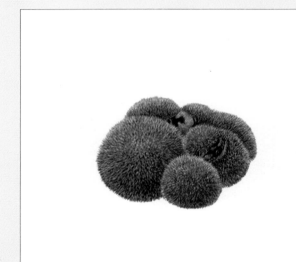

Self-Assessment

Remind children that good readers think about their reading. Have children ask themselves these questions:

- Have I been asking questions and looking for the answers?
- What did I do if I didn't understand something?
- Have I been thinking about what I like or don't like about this story?

25

QuickREFERENCE

Science Link

Tell children that hedgehogs usually sleep during the day and stay awake during the night. Ask if they can name other animals that do this. Prompt discussion by mentioning hamsters, owls, and raccoons.

2 Interact with Literature

Rereading

Literacy Activity Book, p.51

Choices for Rereading

Listen and Read!

Audio Tape for Family Time: *Animal Mothers*

To promote independent reading, place copies of the Little Big Book along with the Audio Tape. Invite children to chime in with the tape as they read the story individually or in small groups.

Students Acquiring English The Audio Tape enables children to hear English as they look at the pictures repeatedly.

Listening for Initial *m*

Have children listen for beginning sounds. Ask children to "meow" each time they hear a word that begins with the sound for *m*. Pause a few times to frame the *m* word and have children identify the initial letter.

Recognizing Language Patterns

LAB, p. 51

As children read the story with you, help them note the language pattern by pointing out that most sentences begin with the word *Mother* followed by an animal's name and how it keeps its baby close. If needed, point out how the pattern changes on pages 20–25.

Provide practice with story language patterns by having children complete *Literacy Activity Book* page 51.

Pantomime the Story

Students Acquiring English Read the story, inviting children to express themselves creatively by pantomiming the animal mothers. Children may wish to use stuffed animals as props or work in small groups to role-play mother and child for animals such as the elephant, zebra, and boar.

Informal Assessment

Use the Story Talk or the retelling activity to assess children's general understanding of the selection.

Additional Support:

- Take children on a "picture walk" through the story and have them tell what is happening on each page.
- Have children cite places where they were confused and reread them with children.

Responding

Choices for Responding

Retelling *Animal Mothers*

Materials
- index cards
- pictures of the animal mothers and their young

Paste pictures of animal mothers and their young onto index cards. Give the picture cards to children, and invite them to retell the story using the picture cards as props.

Students Acquiring English Allow children with limited English proficiency to retell the story in their primary language.

Story Talk

Place children in groups of two or three, and have them respond to one or more of the following:

- Does anything in the story remind you of human babies? What?

- Why do human babies need to stay close to a parent? Why do you think animal babies need to stay close to their parents?

- What other things might animal parents do to take care of their babies?

Personal Response

Invite children to talk about the animal mothers in the selection. What new things did they learn about animal mothers? What surprised them? Ask children to draw a picture of the animal mother and baby that surprised them the most. Encourage them to write or dictate a sentence about their picture.

Comparing Mothers and Babies

Encourage children to look at the illustrations to compare and contrast the animal mothers to their babies. Ask: Which animal babies look just like their mothers? Which look different? How are they different?

3

Instruct and Integrate

Comprehension

Literacy Activity Book, p. 52

Practice Activities

Topic and Details

LAB, p. 52

Help children to recognize details that support the topic and main idea of *Animal Mothers*. First review with them some of the things about animal mothers and their babies that they saw in the story. Then discuss with them some things about animals mothers and their babies that they did <u>not</u> see in the story. *(what the animals eat, how the babies play with each other, how they sleep)* Tell children that those things are not in the story because it is about how animal mothers keep their babies close, not about what the babies eat, or how they play or sleep. Then review with children some of the details that do appear in the story and support the topic and main idea.

Have children complete *Literacy Activity Book* page 52 to show how well they are able to recognize details that do support the topic and main idea of *Animal Mothers*.

Recalling Story Details

Extra Support Place children in groups of three or four. Provide each group with milk-carton die on which pictures of the adult story animals have been pasted. Have children: Roll the die, name the animal shown, and tell how that animal keeps its baby close.

Materials
- empty, pint-size milk cartons
- pictures of animal mothers from the story

Sharing Books

Display several nonfiction picture books about animals and read the titles aloud. Place children in small groups and give a different title to each group. Have children look at the illustrations or photographs to decide what the book is mostly about. Then have groups share their findings with the class. Suggest that each member of the group tell something he or she learned about the animal from the pictures.

Students Acquiring English Children can meet in same-language groups and discuss the books in their primary language and then report in English on what they learned.

Informal Assessment

Note children's ability to identify the topic of a selection and the details that tell more about it.

Phonics/Decoding

Practice Activities

Picture Card Activity

Extra Support Display Picture Cards *monkey, milk, seal.* Name the pictures with children. Explain that you are going to say a sentence about an animal mother and leave out a word. Children can supply the word by saying the picture name that makes sense and begins with the sound for *m*. Read: *A mother _____ teaches her baby.*

Help children understand why *monkey* is the correct choice and why *milk* and *seal* are not. Then repeat the procedure with Picture Cards for *meat, marbles, watermelon* and this sentence: *A mother lion and her cubs like to eat _____.*

Materials
- Picture Cards for *monkey, milk, seal, meat, marbles, watermelon*

Which One Is an *m* Word?

Materials
- Picture Cards for moon and sun.

Display Picture Cards for *moon* and *sun* along the chalkboard ledge as shown. Have children name the pictures and print *m* above the picture whose name begins with the sound for *m*. Then ask children to supply the word.

Busy Families

Have children play the game with partners for practice with *m*/m/ and *s*/s/.

Materials
- Game: Busy Families (See Teacher's Handbook, page H8.)

Portfolio Opportunity

As a record of children's ability to note details, save *Literacy Activity Book* page 52. Save the *m* collage for a record of children's progress with initial consonants.

3

Instruct and Integrate

Phonics/Decoding

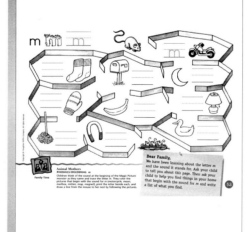

My Big Dictionary

Literacy Activity Book, p. 53

Practice Activities

What's in Mother Kangaroo's Pouch?

Extra Support

- Provide a group of children with a pocket apron and a set of *m* Picture Cards and several other Picture Cards.

- Have one child be the mother kangaroo and wear the apron, putting the Picture Cards in the apron "pouch."

- Children pick a card from the pouch, name the picture, and tell if the picture name begins with the sound for *m*.

Initial *m*

LAB, p. 53

Have children complete *Literacy Activity Book* page 53 to practice identifying words that begin with the sound for *m*.

Home Connection Encourage them to take their pages home to share with family members.

My Big Dictionary

Display pages 22–23 of *My Big Dictionary*. Read the words on page 22 aloud to children, pointing to the initial *m* and emphasizing the sound /m/ as you read. Then invite partners to work together to find five things on page 23 that begin with the sound for *m*. You may want to encourage children to use temporary spellings and make a list of their words for their Journals.

Informal Assessment

Note children's ability to identify words that begin with the sound for *m* as they complete the activities on this page. Also observe whether children can match spoken words to printed words.

Concepts About Print

Practice Activities

Reading a Poem

Audio Tape for Family Time:
Animal Mothers

Extra Support On the poster invite children to listen as you read *Travel Plans* again. Recall with children that a word is a group of letters. Frame the first group of letters and explain that it is the word *If.* Then read the poem line for line, calling on volunteers to frame the words as you read them.

Place copies of the Little Big Book along with the Audio Tape. Have children match spoken words to print by pointing to each word as the narrator reads.

"M" Is for Mother Collage

Invite children to make a collage of things a human mother might give her child. Children can cut out pictures of *m* words from old magazines or draw pictures to include on their collages. Encourage children to label the items on their collages.

3

Instruct and Integrate

Vocabulary

Vocabulary Expansion

Specific Words

Help children expand their vocabularies, by pausing before reading the following pages and asking children to listen for specific words.

page 6	Listen for a word that names a baby lion. (cub)
page 8	Listen for a word that means "holds tightly." (clings)
page 13	Listen for a word that names a baby koala. (cub)
page 16	Listen for a word that names a baby kangaroo. (joey)
page 19	Listen for a word that names an animal body part. (trunk)
page 20	Listen for a word that names a baby zebra. (foal)
page 22	Listen for a word that means "small group." (bunch)

Students Acquiring English To support their understanding, help children to point out in the illustration each thing named.

Animals and Their Babies

Remind children that some of the animal babies in the story had special names. List these names on chart paper. If some children made a list of animal baby names from the story, ask them to help you with the class chart.

Challenge Discuss the chart with children. Encourage them to name other animals who have babies with special names. Add the animals to the list as they are suggested. Invite children to illustrate the chart.

Informal Assessment

As children complete the activities, note whether or not they exhibit familiarity with story vocabulary. Also observe whether they can listen for details.

Listening

Listening Activities

Learning About Animal Fathers

Explain to children that in many animal families, it is the animal mother that takes care of the babies. It is usually the animal father's job to protect the family. Then guide children in talking about other animal families to highlight the role of animal fathers. You might share these facts with children:

1. Most mother and father birds work together to build a nest for their families. After the mother bird lays her eggs, the parents take turns sitting on the eggs to keep them warm. When the baby birds hatch, both parents are kept busy watching over their chicks and finding food for them.

2. The father seahorse has a special pouch on its stomach. He carries the seahorse eggs and protects them until they hatch.

3. The small mouth black bass father makes a nest for his family by using his tail to "dig" a hole in the sand. After the mother fish lays the eggs, he guards them by swimming back and forth over the eggs until they hatch. He won't even let the mother fish come close!

Name That Animal

Invite children to play an animal guessing game. Have pairs take turns choosing an animal from *Animal Mothers,* keeping the name secret, but describing it to a partner. Partners should listen carefully for details that will help them name the animal being described.

Listen and Learn

Invite children to learn more about animal families. Share with them the following audio-visual material:

- Pets and Their Wild Relatives, *National Geographic:* F&V

3

Instruct and Integrate

Oral Language

Choices for Oral Language

How Might These Mothers Act?

Display photographs of a gorilla and a dog. Encourage children to name the animals and describe them. Ask them to guess how each animal mother might keep its baby close. You might guide their thinking by asking questions such as:

- Which animal from the story is a gorilla most like? How do you think a mother gorilla keeps its baby close?

- Which animal from the story is a dog most like? How do you think a mother dog keeps its puppy close?

Display the pages from the story that correspond to children's responses. Help them use the language pattern in the story to state their ideas.

> A mother gorilla carries her baby in her arms.
>
> A mother dog carries her puppy in her mouth.

Animal Parents

Display the Animal Parents poster and help children identify the animal parents and their young. Then invite them to describe the animals and discuss how each parent might keep their children close.

Dramatic Play

Using a doll, have volunteers show different ways human parents keep their babies close. Prompt the children observing to tell how the doll was handled: How did (child's name) hold the doll? How is this different from the way (child's name) held it?

Poster

Animal Parents

Elephant and Calf

Polar Bear and Cub

Meerkat and Cubs

Deer and Fawn

Informal Assessment

Note children's skill with theme-related vocabulary. Also observe whether they try to sound out or copy words for writing activities.

 # Writing

Choices for Writing

People Keep Their Babies Close, Too!

Review some of the ways that animal mothers keep their babies close. Then invite children to brainstorm ways in which human mothers and fathers keep their babies close. Print the ideas on chart paper. Then read the list with children. Encourage them to illustrate the list with drawings or pictures cut from magazines.

Ways Human Mothers Keep Their Babies Close

- baby stroller
- carrying them in their arms
- baby carriage

Picture/Word Wall

Help children begin a Picture/Word Wall of animal pictures labeled with animal names. If children began such a list in the previous unit, encourage them to add any new animals to it at this time.

Our Book of Animal Babies

 Students Acquiring English Invite children to make animal baby books. Have them work in small mixed-language groups to decide what animal babies they will include. Children can then draw pictures of the animal babies and refer to the chart to label their pictures. After binding the pages together, have groups exchange and read each other's books.

Portfolio Opportunity

Invite children to save their animal baby books.

Cross-Curricular Activities

Science

More About Animal Families

Challenge Display the books and read their titles aloud. Note that all the books tell more about animals. Invite groups of children to choose a title and look at the book's illustrations to learn more about one of the animals. Encourage them to share their findings with the class.

Materials
- nonfiction picture books of animals

Social Studies

Where in the World?

Materials
- world map
- pictures of the animal mothers and their young
- yarn or string

★★★ **Multicultural Link** Help children create a bulletin board display around a world map to show where the different animals in the selection live:

Africa–lion, elephant, zebra, baboon, chimpanzee, hedgehog

Central and South America–sloth

Australia–koala, kangaroo

Europe/Asia–wild boar, hedgehog

This is also a good opportunity for children from other countries to tell about the animals from their countries. They may need to talk with family members first before relaying the information to the class.

Creative Movement

Walk Like the Animals

Invite children to pantomime walking or moving like the animals in the story. For example, children might stalk or arch their backs like cats, sway like elephants, or hop like kangaroos. Then challenge children to walk or move like these animals:

duck	rabbit	frog
crab	bird	snake

Math

Sorting Animals

- Remind children that the animal mothers are alike because they all keep their babies close, but they are different because they have different ways of doing that.

- Display the animal pictures and brainstorm with children other ways in which the animals are alike and different. Call on volunteers to sort the pictures accordingly.

- Help children create charts to record their findings.

Students Acquiring English Compare-and-contrast activities help children develop concepts. Encourage children to draw pictures of the similarities and the differences in their charts.

Materials
- chart paper
- tape
- multiple pictures of the animal mothers and their young

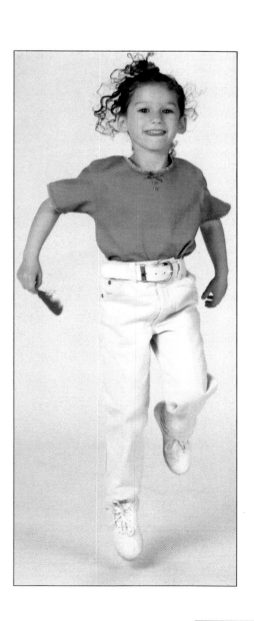

BIG BOOK
SELECTION:
Me Too!

Big Book

Little Big Book

● **Best Books For Children**

by Mercer Mayer

Other Books by the Author

A Boy, a Dog, and a Frog

There's an Alligator Under My Bed

What Do You Do with a Kangaroo?

Selection Summary

In this story, Mercer Mayer's main character faces a problem many older siblings have — his little sister wants to do everything he does. While big brother is patient, his frustration is apparent as he responds to his sister's repeated "Me too!" requests by letting her join in his fun. His patience finally pays off when he wants to share her candy cane, and she lets him.

Lesson Planning Guide

	Skill/Strategy Instruction	Meeting Individual Needs	Lesson Resources
1 **Introduce** *the* **Literature** *Pacing: 1 day*	**Shared Reading and Writing** Warm-up/Build Background, T156 Shared Reading, T156 Shared Writing, T157	Choices for Rereading, T157	**Poster** My Family, T156 *Literacy Activity Book* Personal Response, p. 54
2 **Interact** *with* **Literature** *Pacing: 1–2 days*	**Reading Strategies** Self-Question, T158 Monitor, T158, T162 Evaluate, T158, T160, T168 Think About Words, T166 **Minilessons** ✔ High-Frequency Word: *my,* T159 ✔ High-Frequency Word: *said,* T165 ✔ Initial s, T161 ✔ Fantasy/Realism, T163 ✔ Matches Spoken Words to Print, T167	**Students Acquiring English,** T158, T159, T162, T165, T171 **Extra Support,** T160, T163, T164, T166, T168 **Challenge,** T161, T169 **Rereading and Responding,** T170-T171	*Literacy Activity Book* Language Patterns, p. 55 **Picture, Letter, and Word Cards,** T159, T161, T165, T167 **Story Retelling Props,** T171, H5 **Audio Tape** for Family Time: *Me Too!* T170 See the Houghton Mifflin **Internet** resources for additional activities
3 **Instruct** *and* **Integrate** *Pacing: 1–2 days*	**Reading/Listening Center,** Comprehension, T172 Phonics/Decoding, T173-T174 Concepts About Print, T175 Vocabulary, T176 Listening, T177 **Independent Reading & Writing,** T178-T179 **Language/Writing Center,** Oral Language, T180 Writing, T181 **Cross-Curricular Center,** Cross-Curricular Activities, T182-T183	**Extra Support,** T172, T173, T175 **Students Acquiring English,** T174, T182 **Challenge,** T177, T183	*Literacy Activity Book* Comprehension, p. 57-58 Phonics/Decoding, p. 59 Vocabulary, p. 60 Tear-and-Take, p. 61-62 **Picture, Letter, and Word Cards,** T173, T176 **My Big Dictionary,** T173 **Audio Tape** for Family Time: *Me, Too!,* T177 See the Houghton Mifflin **Internet** resources for additional activities

✔ *Indicates Tested Skills. See page T103 for assessment options.*

1

Introduce *the* Literature

Shared Reading and Writing

Poster

MY FAMILY

Part of my family
is grown-up and tall.
Part of my family
is little and small.
I'm in the middle
and pleased
with them all.

MARCHETTE CHUTE

DAD
Mom
ME
BABY
MY DOG

Poster: Family Time

INTERACTIVE LEARNING

Warm-up/Build Background

Sharing Poetry

- Read aloud "My Family" on the poster.

- Have children look at the illustration. Ask: Who is "grown-up and tall"? (Mom, Dad) Who is "little and small"? (Baby) Who is "in the middle?" (Me—the girl)

- Ask children who in their own families is "grown-up and tall," "little and small," and, possibly, "in the middle."

- Help children see the varying abilities of family members by discussing the sister and little brother on the poster. You may want to use these prompts:

  What things might this sister and brother do together?

  What might the sister be able to do that her little brother cannot do? (Sample answer: paint a picture)

  What might happen if the little brother tried to do one of these things?

- Encourage children to join in as you read the poem again.

Shared Reading
LAB, p. 54

Preview and Predict

- Display *Me Too!* Point to and read aloud the title and the author/illustrator's name.

- Briefly discuss the cover illustration. Ask children to tell who they think the characters are and why one of the characters might be crying.

- Display and read aloud pages 2–3 of the story. Call on a volunteer to point out the storyteller and the little sister. Help children identify the characters as needed.

- Take a "picture walk" through page 9, inviting children to describe the scenes. Ask them to predict what the story will be about. Encourage them to predict other things the little sister might want to do like her brother.

Read Together
- Read the story together, encouraging children to join in with the words they know. Encourage children to supply the words "Me too!" whenever they occur in the story.

  - As you read, pause occasionally to allow children to comment on the illustrations and to predict what will happen next.

  - Pause after page 23 to ask what children think the little sister will say to her brother. Then read to the end of the story to find out if their predictions are correct.

Personal Response

Have children complete *Literacy Activity Book* page 54 to show which of the things the brother and sister did that they too would like to do.

 ## Shared Writing: *New Scene for the Story*

Brainstorming

Invite children to write a new scene for the story. Have them suggest more things that the big brother does that the little sister also wants to do. Have children choose one of their favorites to write about. Then make a word web to generate ideas for the new scene.

More Me Too Ideas
1. bike riding
★ 2. paint a picture
3. play the piano
4. go to school
5. make a peanut butter sandwich

big brother is painting

little sister says "Me too!"

★ PAINT A PICTURE

sister gets paint all over the table

Drafting

Have volunteers contribute sentences to the class scene. Record their suggestions on chart paper.

Publishing and Sharing

Have volunteers illustrate the new scene to go with the text. Then display children's work on a bulletin board.

Choices for Rereading

Suggestions for rereading are provided on page T170. These include:
- Noting Language Patterns
- Fantasy and Realism
- Listen and Read!

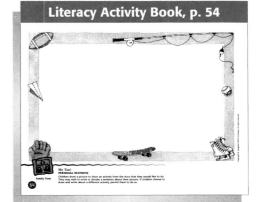
Literacy Activity Book, p. 54

Interact *with* Literature

2

Then I had to help her ride.

4

Reading Strategies

► **Monitor**
Self-Question
Evaluate

Student Application Discuss how good listeners and readers think about what happens in a story so they will understand it. Recall with children the questions they might ask to help them understand a story. (Does this make sense? Is this something I would do? Is this what I thought would happen?) Then help children develop a list of questions for the story.

Purpose Setting

Tell children to read the story with you to see if their questions are answered. Help them use words and picture clues to understand the story.

QuickREFERENCE

Visual Literacy

Point out the speech balloon on page 2. Elicit that the "balloon" tells what the little sister is saying. Ask children where they've seen balloons like this to show what a person is thinking or saying. (comic strips, cartoons, advertisements)

Students Acquiring English

Syntax Encourage children with limited English proficiency to develop a list of questions in their language to help them understand the story.

3

I had a paper airplane
that I made myself.
But my little sister
saw it and said...

Me too!

MINILESSON

Vocabulary

High-Frequency Word: *my*

TESTED SKILL

Teach/Model

Display the Word Card *my*.

Reread the opening sentence on page 2. Point to word card *my* and read it for children. Ask:

• How many letters are in *my*?

• What letter does *my* begin with? End with?

Have volunteers find and frame the word *my* twice on page 2. If a child points to the word *me*, compare the two words, noting that they are almost the same but that the last letters are different.

Practice/Apply

Ask children to find and frame the words *my* on page 5. Then reread the page with children, pausing for them to supply the High-Frequency Word.

SKILL FINDER My and Said, p. T176

Phonics/Decoding Review

Reread page 5, asking children to raise their hands each time they hear a word that begins like *mother* and *monster*. *(made, myself, my, me)* Frame each word and have the initial letter named.

Students Acquiring English
MEETING INDIVIDUAL NEEDS

Word Meanings Remind children that they can figure out vocabulary by using picture clues. Invite a volunteer to point out the skateboard (page 2) and the paper airplane (page 5).

Interact
with
Literature

Reading Strategies

▶ **Evaluate**

After reading through page 9, pause to ask children how they feel about the story so far. Use the following prompts as needed:

- Do you like the story so far? Why or why not?

- Do you think this is the way real brothers and sisters sometimes act?

Encourage children to share any other feelings or opinions they may have about the story up to this point.

Then she threw it in a tree.

6

I went hiking with my friends and my little sister said, "Me too!"

8

Quick REFERENCE

 Journal

As children read the story, have them draw an item or write a word to help them remember each activity the little sister wanted to do. Suggest that they write the words "Me too!" under those activities that also appeal to them.

 Extra Support

Help children understand the meaning of *hiking*. Have them use context and picture clues to conclude that *hiking* is "taking a long walk." Invite children to name places where they like to go hiking.

7

I had to carry her because she got tired.

Me too! Me too!

9

Challenge

MEETING INDIVIDUAL NEEDS

Have children tell what the animal in the water on page 9 might be. (frog, turtle, or snake) Ask them what other animals are found in water. (fish, beavers, bugs, lizards, ducks)

Phonics/Decoding

Initial s

TESTED SKILL

Teach/Model

Display Magic Picture *seal.* Tell children that Magic Picture *seal* can help them remember the sound for *s.* Have children say *seal* listening for the beginning sound. Then read aloud the sentence on page 8, asking children to listen for two words that begin with the same sound as *seal.* Frame *sister* and then *said.* Ask children to name the first letter in each word.

Now, have children say *said, sister,* and *seal,* listening for the beginning sounds.

Practice/Apply

Display the following sentence:

My little sister said, "Me too!"

Read the sentence with children, pausing for them to read the word *said.* Then reread the sentence, asking children to clap when they hear a word that begins like *said* and *seal.* Frame *sister* and underline the initial *s.*

SKILL FINDER — Decoding *s* Words, p. T173

Interact *with* Literature

Reading Strategies

▶ Monitor

Display pages 10–11 and reread the text to children. Ask: Does it make sense that the brother and his friends had to be careful when little sister played football with them?

Encourage children to use clues in the words and pictures to better understand this page. You might prompt discussion by asking:

- What are the brother and his friends wearing to play football? (helmets) Why are they wearing helmets? (So they don't get hurt when they play.)

- Does the little sister have a helmet? (no) How can this help us understand why the brother and his friends have to be careful?

10

12

QuickREFERENCE

Science Link

Have children use picture clues to tell what time of year is shown on pages 12–13. (winter) Invite children to identify the seasons shown in other story illustrations.

MEETING INDIVIDUAL NEEDS
Students Acquiring English

Word Meaning The word *football* may confuse children from other countries where the word names the game of soccer. Tell children that in the United States, people play two kinds of "football," soccer and the football shown in the picture.

11

Guess what my little sister said.

13

Comprehension

Fantasy/
Realism

TESTED SKILL

Teach/Model

Note with children that *A Birthday Basket for Tía* told about real people and how they act and that *Animal Mothers* told about real animals and how they act. Ask children how this story is different. (It tells about animal-like characters that act like people.)

Think Aloud

When I read a story, I think about whether the story tells about real or make-believe things. In this story, the characters act like human brothers and sisters, but they are not people. They look like animals, but I know that they are not real animals. Real animals do not talk, wear clothes, or play games.

Practice/Apply

Invite children to name things in the story that the characters do. Ask if these are things that real animals could do. Ask if they are things that human brothers and sisters could do.

SKILL FINDER

Fantasy/Realism in Theme Stories, p. T172

Minilessons, See Themes 6; 10

Extra Support

MEETING INDIVIDUAL NEEDS

Children who have never seen snow or been sledding may not realize what the brother is planning to do, or why the sister is so eager to join in. You may wish to explain sledding to children.

I went skating on the pond.
My little sister said, "Me too!"
She doesn't know how to skate,
so I had to hold her up.

Me too!

14

There was one last piece of cake.
My little sister said…

Me too!

16

QuickREFERENCE

Science Link

Mention that in many parts of the country the winter months are very cold. The cold temperatures often cause water, like the water in the pond, to freeze. Use the example of making ice cubes in a freezer to help illustrate this concept.

 MEETING INDIVIDUAL NEEDS

Extra Support

Children living in warmer climates may not be familiar with ice skating. Point out the ice skates on pages 14–15. Ask children to compare these skates to those they would wear to skate on a sidewalk. (roller skates, in-line skates)

15

I had to cut it in half,
even though I saw it first.

17

Vocabulary

High-Frequency Words: *said*

TESTED SKILL

Teach/Model

Display Picture Card *seal.* Have children name the picture and tell what it helps them remember. (the sound for *s*) Then display Word Card *said* and have the initial consonant identified. Ask what sound this word begins with. (the sound for *s*) Point to Word Card *said* and read it for children. Then read the sentence on page 16. Have volunteers find and frame the word *said* on page 16. If a child points to the word *sister,* compare the two words, noting that only the beginning letters are the same.

Practice/Apply

Ask children to find and frame the word *said* on page 18. Then reread the page with children, pausing for them to supply the high-frequency word.

SKILL FINDER

My and Said, p. T176

Math Link

Ask how the brother shared the cake with his sister. (He cut it in half.) Note with children that when something is cut in half, it is divided into two parts that are the same size.

MEETING INDIVIDUAL NEEDS
Students Acquiring English

Word Meaning Use pictures to show the meaning of *pond.* Note that the pond in the picture is frozen, but during warmer weather people might swim or fish in it. Show children pictures of other bodies of water: ocean, river, lake.

Me Too!

THEME: FAMILY TIME

Interact *with* Literature

When I went fishing she said, "Me too!" Then she caught the biggest fish.

18

I went to my secret tree house. My little sister said…

Me too!

Mom said I had to help her up.

20

Reading Strategies

▶ **Think About Words**

Display page 20 and discuss how children can figure out the word *Mom.*

The story says: *I went to my secret tree house. My little sister said, "Me too!" _____ said I had to help her up.*

- **What makes sense** Point out that two people who might make the big brother do something to help his sister are *Dad* and *Mom.*

- **Sounds for letters** Point to the word *Mom,* noting that it begins with the letter *m.* Ask children to say the words *Dad* and *Mom,* listening for the beginning sound. Ask which word begins with the sound for *m.*

- **Picture clues** Note with children that only the big brother and his little sister are in the picture and that they can't be the ones who said big brother had to help little sister up to the tree house. Mom isn't in the picture, so she could be the one who wants big brother to help her.

Have children reread the sentence with you to see if *Mom* makes sense.

QuickREFERENCE

Math Link

Ask who caught the biggest fish on pages 18 and 19. (the little sister) Display three books of varying sizes and have children place them in size order. Use the words *big, bigger,* and *biggest* to describe the books.

MEETING INDIVIDUAL NEEDS **Extra Support**

If necessary, help children understand that *my* and *My* are the same word; they both begin with the letter *m* and end with the letter *y.*

Phonemic Awareness Review

Invite children to listen as you reread the text on page 21. Ask them to listen to find the two words that rhyme. *(do, too)* Encourage children to name other words that rhyme with *do* and *too.*

19

Everything I do
my little sister says,
"Me too!"

21

Concepts About Print

Matches Spoken Words to Print

Teach/Model

TESTED SKILL

Display Word Cards *my* and *said* along the chalkboard ledge.

| my | said |

Explain that you will say one of the words. Say: *said.* Have a volunteer hold up that word card.

Then say *my* and choose another volunteer to hold up that word card. Repeat the procedure to allow for other volunteers.

Then display this sentence on the board, and read it aloud:

My little sister saw me and said, "Me too!"

Have volunteers identify the words *my* and *said* in the sentence. Make sure children don't confuse *my* with *me,* or *said* with *sister* or *saw.*

Practice/Apply

Reread pages from the story asking volunteers to identify *my* and *said* in the sentences. Have children match the Word Cards to the words *my* and *said* in the story.

SKILL FINDER Play "Me Too!", p. T175

1 look   3 is
2 see   4 can
3 the   I
* a   1 my*
4 at   2 said
1 find
2 has

Interact
with
Literature

Reading Strategies

▶ Evaluate

Tell children that good readers and listeners think about the most important parts of a story because they will help them remember it.

Children also tell whether or not they liked the story. Encourage children to take turns retelling the story and tell how they feel about it.

Today my little sister had a candy cane of her very own.

22

Guess what my little sister said.

You too!

24

Self-Assessment

Encourage children to think about their reading by asking themselves these questions:

- Was any part of the story confusing to me? If so, what part?
- What did I do to help myself understand what I was reading?

Quick**REFERENCE**

Technology Link

Children who liked *Me Too!* may also enjoy exploring a CD-ROM interactive experience based on Mercer Mayer's *Just Grandma and Me* (Broderbund Software).

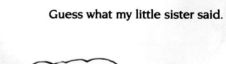

Extra Support

Ask how the "Me too" in the speech balloon on page 23 differs from the other "Me toos" in the story. (It ends with a different mark.) Tell children that this marks turns it into a question to show that the brother isn't sure if his sister will share.

Big Book p. 23

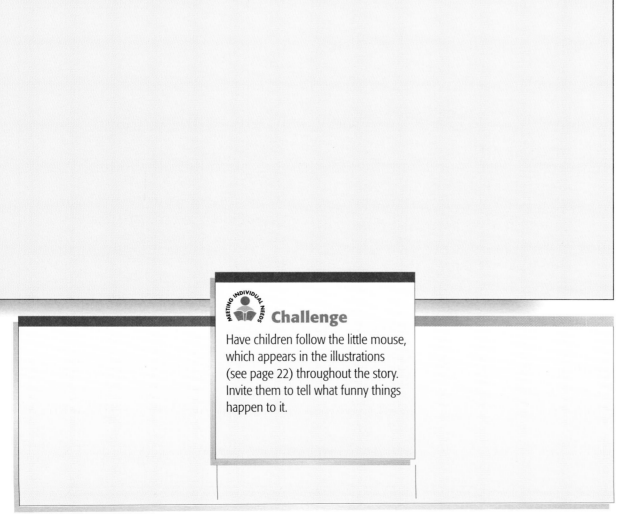

Challenge

Have children follow the little mouse, which appears in the illustrations (see page 22) throughout the story. Invite them to tell what funny things happen to it.

2 Interact with Literature

Rereading

Literacy Activity Book, p. 55

Choices for Rereading

Fantasy and Realism

Read the story to help children distinguish between reality and fantasy. Pause now and then to ask questions about the characters and what they are doing:

- Pages 8–9: Do real animals wear clothes? (no) Can real animals be friends with other animals? (yes)

- Pages 12–13: Point out the brother and sister's tree house and ask: Can real animals live in trees? (yes) Do real animals live in trees that have doors and windows? (no)

- Pages 16–17: Do real animals have paws and fur? (yes) Do real animals eat with forks? (no)

Listen and Read!

 **Audio Tape** for Family Time: *Me Too!*

To promote independent reading, place copies of the Little Big Book along with the Audio Tape. Invite children to chime in with the tape as they read the story individually or in small groups.

Noting Language Patterns

LAB, p. 55

Invite children to read the story with you to note the language pattern. Mention that each time the brother tries to do something, the little sister says "Me too!" Pause for children to read these words and to chime in on the "my little sister said" phrases.

Then have children complete *Literacy Activity Book* page 55 to practice the language pattern.

Informal Assessment

Use the Story Talk or the retelling activity to assess children's general understanding of the selection.

Additional Support:

- Reread confusing parts of the story with children.

- Help children find story and picture details that help answer their questions.

Responding

Choices for Responding

Retelling *Me Too!*

Provide pairs with the story pieces and poster for *Me Too!*
Invite them to role play the brother and little sister in the
story. Have the brother choose a piece, place it on the appropriate spot on the poster, and role-play the story scene in
which it appears. Have the little sister respond by saying "Me too!" When
children come to the candy cane piece, make sure they reverse the roles
with the brother saying "Me too" and the sister saying "You too."

> **Materials**
> - Story Retelling Props
>   (See Teacher's Handbook,
>   page H5.)

Story Talk

Place children in groups of two or three,
and have them respond to the following:

- If you were the big brother what
  would you do? Would you let your
  little sister play with you? Why or
  why not?

- Do you know anyone who is like the
  big brother? The little sister? How are
  the people you know like the story
  characters? How are they different?

- Who are you most like—the big
  brother or the big sister?

Students Acquiring English You may
want to put children with limited English
proficiency in same-language groups for
this activity.

Create a New Scene

Briefly discuss the end of the story with
children. Have them think of other
things the little sister might do that the
big brother would also want to do.
Suggest that children draw pictures to
illustrate their ideas and write the words
"Me too" on the drawings. Children
might enjoy telling what happens when
the big brother joins in on the little
sister's fun.

Portfolio Opportunity

Save children's "New Scenes" as a
sample of their response to the literature.
Also keep *Literacy Activity Book* page 55
for a record of how well they understand
the language pattern in the story.

Instruct *and* Integrate

Comprehension

Literacy Activity Book, p. 57

Practice Activities

Fantasy / Realism in Theme Stories

LAB, p. 57

Display the theme books and read their titles aloud. Encourage children to briefly recall the stories. Then ask:

- Which book tells us about real animal families? (*Animal Mothers*)
- Which book has real characters that show how families might act? (*A Birthday Basket for Tía*)
- Which book tells a story about make-believe characters? (*Me Too!*)

Briefly review the things in *Me Too!* that make it a make-believe story. (the animals talk, wear clothes, behave in a way that real animals do not) Then have children complete *Literacy Activity Book* page 57 to show how well they are able to distinguish between fantasy and realism in *Me Too!*

Picture Clues

Display several picture books from the bibliography, and read the titles aloud. Arrange children in small groups, and give each group a book. Ask the group to look for picture clues to help to predict if the story tells about things that could really happen or if it tells about make-believe things. Have children justify their predictions by noting details in the pictures. Then ask children to listen as you read one or two of the stories. What clues in the words help tell if the story is real or make-believe?

Make-Believe Characters

 Extra Support Mention to children that in some make-believe stories, people do things that they could not really do in real life. Show this by asking:

- Could real children fly in an airplane? Could real children fly on a magic carpet?
- Could real children keep pet elephants in their bedrooms? Could real children keep pet hamsters in their bedrooms?

Invite children to pose similar questions. Have them work in pairs to draw two pictures, one real and one make-believe.

Informal Assessment

As children complete the activities, note their ability to distinguish between fantasy and realism. Also observe how well they can decode and spell words beginning with the letter *s*.

Phonics/Decoding

Practice Activities

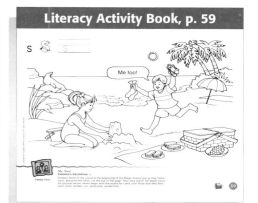

Decoding *s* Words

Materials
- Picture Cards for *sandwich, pancakes, sink; soap, piano, seesaw*

Extra Support Display Picture Cards *sandwich, pancakes, sink* and name the pictures with children. Then explain that you are going to say a sentence that tells more about the brother and his sister and leave out one of the words. Children can supply the missing word by saying a picture name that makes sense and begins with the sound for *s*. Read: *I wanted to eat my _____. "Me too!" said my little sister.*

Discuss why *sandwich* is the correct choice and why *pancakes* and *sink* are not. Then repeat the procedure with the Picture Cards for *soap, piano, seesaw* and the sentence: *My friends and I were playing on the _____.*

Initial *s*

LAB, p. 59

Have children complete *Literacy Activity Book* page 59 to practice identifying words that begin with the sound for *s*.

Find *s* Words

Display pages 32–35 of *My Big Dictionary*. Read the words *sailboat, salad, sandbox,* and *sandwich* on page 32, *seal* and *sing* on page 33, and *soccer* and *sun* on page 34, pointing to the letter *s* and emphasizing /s/ as you read. Invite partners to work together to find five things they see on page 35 that begin with the sound for *s*. Encourage children to use temporary spellings and list their words in their Journals.

My Big Dictionary

Portfolio Opportunity

For a record of children's ability to decode *s* words, save *Literacy Activity Book* page 59. Also keep their pictures of make-believe and real characters as a record of how well they distinguish between fantasy and realism.

3

Instruct *and* Integrate

Phonics/Decoding

Practice Activities

My Secret Tree House

Sketch a tree house on a large sheet of paper and mount it on a bulletin board. Remind children that the big brother had a secret tree house like this. Have children say *secret,* listening for the beginning sound. Display the word *secret* and underline the *s.* Invite children to draw or cut from magazines pictures whose names begin with *s* to paste in the tree house.

Students Acquiring English For this activity, you might pair up native speakers with children who are learning English. Later ask them to identify, using English, the pictures they found with their partners. Label the pictures in English. Then ask children to identify these words in their primary language for the class.

A Picture Book for Little Sister

Suggest that one thing the big brother in *Me Too!* might do for his sister is make her a picture book. Provide children with drawing paper and invite them to make an "s" picture book for the little sister. Encourage them to label the pictures they draw.

Spelling *m* and *s* Words

Shuffle the following Picture Cards and display them along the chalkboard ledge: *mouse, mask, milk, moon, mop, saw, seal, sink, soap, sun.* Name the pictures with children. Then have them help you spell the name of each Picture Card by supplying the initial consonant as you write the words on the board.

Materials

- Picture Cards for *mouse, mask, milk, moon, mop, saw, seal, sink, soap, sun*

Informal Assessment

As children complete the activities, note the ease with which they are able to recognize and identify words that begin with *s.* Also observe how well children match the spoken words *my* and *said* to the written words.

Concepts About Print

Practice Activities

Play "Me Too!"

Extra Support Make multiple word cards for *my* and *said* and distribute one card to each child. Then invite children to play "Me Too!"

- Hold up a Word Card, such as *my*, so that children can see it. Say: I have the Word Card *my*.

- Ask children to read their word cards. If they have the one that says *my*, they should respond by holding it up and saying "Me too!"

- Repeat the procedure with the word *said*.

- Have children exchange word cards to play again.

Listening for *My* and *Said*

Have children follow along as you read the story. Encourage volunteers to find and point to the words *my* and *said* when they hear them read.

Instruct and Integrate

Vocabulary

Literacy Activity Book, p. 60

High-Frequency Words

My and Said
LAB, p. 60

- Provide partners with Word Cards: *my, said.*
- Have children place the cards face down on a table top.
- Have them take turns choosing a word card, reading the word, and using it in an oral sentence.
- Have children complete *Literacy Activity Book* page 60 to practice reading the High-Frequency Words.

Reading *My* and *Said* Sentences

Display Word Cards *my* and *said,* and have them read by children. Then demonstrate how you can use Word and Picture cards to create sentences:

| My | | said | |

Have children read the sentences. Then invite them to create their own sentences using the Word and Picture Cards.

My Own Things

Invite children to make books titled *My Own Things.* Provide each child with several sheets of drawing paper and ask them to write and draw pictures to complete sentences that tell about their own things. Provide children with the following sentence frame:

My _____ , said (child's name.)

Bind the drawings together to form individual books. Then have children read their books aloud to classmates.

Tear-and-Take Story
LAB, p. 61–62

Have children remove *Literacy Activity Book* page 61, fold it to make a book, and read the story.

Home Connection Suggest that children take their books home and read them to family members.

My Family

Listening

Listening Activities

Ask the Characters

- Have children brainstorm a list of questions they might like to ask the big brother or the little sister.

- Record their suggestions on chart paper.

- Have children take turns role-playing the big brother or little sister to answer the questions of you, the interviewer.

Challenge Invite children to take the role of the interviewer and the little mouse seen in the illustrations. Have the interviewer ask the mouse questions about its involvement in and view of story incidents. Encourage children to be creative.

Listen for "Me Too!"

Audio Tape for Family Time: *Me Too!*

Invite children to listen for the phrase *Me Too!* as they play the Audio Tape. They might want to make a tally mark on paper each time they hear it and then count the total number of times the phrase occurs in the story.

More Stories

Share other books by Mercer Mayer, such as *A Boy, A Dog, and a Frog* or *There's an Alligator Under My Bed.*

Portfolio Opportunity

For a record of children's recognition of the high-frequency words, save their *My Own Things* books. You may also wish to record individuals reading the Tear-and-Take stories.

3

Instruct *and* Integrate

Independent Reading & Writing

Snow Fun

WATCH **ME** READ

Snow Fun
by Connie Hubert

This story provides practice and application for the following skills:

■ **High-Frequency Words:** *My, Said*

■ **Phonics/Decoding Skills:** Initial *m* and *s*

INTERACTIVE LEARNING

Independent Reading
Watch Me Read

Preview and Predict	• Display *Snow Fun.* Point to and read the title and the author's name.
	• Briefly discuss the cover illustration. Have children predict what the girl in the picture might want to do in the snow.
	• Take a "picture walk" through the first seven pages of the story. Encourage children to discuss the pictures. Note the rebuses used in the story sentences and identify them for children: *sunglasses, Mother, buttons, Grandmother, crayon, Sister, mittens, Brother, scarf, Father, hat, Grandfather, snowman, Baby.*
	• Invite children to predict what the "fun" will be.
Read the Story	• Have children read the story independently to find out if their predictions about *Snow Fun* are correct.
	• After reading the story ask: What was the winter surprise? Is this how you thought the story would end?
Rereading	• **Cooperative Reading** Invite children to form groups of seven to reread the story. Suggest that each child assume a character and read aloud what that character says.
	• **Noting Details** Have children reread the story with partners to find the rebus objects in the art. Suggest that one child read the words, while the other scans the picture for the object.
Responding	• **Personal Response** Invite children to tell what they liked best about the family's snowman.
	• **My Own Snowman** Invite children to draw snowmen they'd like to make. Suggest they use the language pattern from the story to label their picture: "My [REBUS: snowman]," said (Child's name).

Informal Assessment

As children read aloud *Snow Fun and* complete other activities, note the ease with which they recognize the high-frequency words. Also observe whether children use any story words in their written responses.

Student Selected Reading

Books for the Library Corner

Display the Books for the Library Corner suggested in the Bibliography in a special place in the classroom. Encourage children to explore these titles during scheduled reading time as well as independent leisure time.

Books for Teacher Read Aloud and Shared Reading

Encourage children to select a theme-related title for you to read to them or with them. You might ask a different child each day to choose a book. Or, you might select a title that is appropriate for a particular classroom experience.

Student Selected Writing

Reading Logs

Suggest that children keep reading logs. During scheduled writing time, encourage them to respond to the family stories and poems they hear and read by drawing and writing their thoughts. Foster independent writing by suggesting that children use invented spellings, but do offer assistance as needed.

Sharing and Reflecting

Provide time for children to share their *Family Time* writings with their classmates. Feature different child authors each day by asking children to choose their favorite works for duplication. Authors may enjoy assisting in the copying of the works, as well as passing out the copies for class reading.

Books for Independent Reading

Encourage children to choose their own books. They might choose one of the following titles.

Animal Mothers
by Atsushi Komori

Me Too!
by Mercer Mayer

Have students reread this selection silently or aloud to a partner.

See the Bibliography on pages T98–T99 for more theme-related books for independent reading.

Ideas for Independent Writing

Encourage children to write on self-selected topics. For those who need help getting started, suggest one of the following activities:

- A "I Like You" **note** to a friend or family member
- A **caption** for a family photograph
- An **invitation** to a Family Get-Together

Portfolio Opportunity

Save examples of the writing children do independently on self-selected topics.

3

Instruct *and* Integrate

Oral Language

Choices for Oral Language

Outdoor Games

Recall with children some of the activities the brother in *Me Too!* enjoyed doing. Mention to children that many of these activities need special equipment. Ask children to name activities they enjoy. As activities are suggested, list them on chart paper. Discuss each one and add to the chart any special things needed for the activity. Invite children to illustrate the finished list.

Game	Special Things
Football	football, helmet
Fishing	fishing pole
Ice Skating	ice skates
Baseball	baseball, bat, mitt
Soccer	soccer ball
Hopscotch	sidewalk, chalk, marker
Roller Skating	roller skates, knee pads, elbow pads, helmet

Asking "Me Too"

Being left out is something no child likes. Help children practice polite ways to ask "Me too" to join in a group's fun. Using the names of your children, invite them to act out scenes similar to those below. Have children tell how they would politely ask to join the group, and have the group members respond in kind:

- Amy and Mark are building a block tower. Jess wants to help.

- Tasso, Kevin, and Amanda are painting. Lee and Bryan want to paint, too.

- Joe, Dina, and Mario are playing dominoes. Wendy wants to play, too.

Mention that sometimes people are afraid to ask if they can join in. How would children invite these people to join them?

Things People Say

Display the phrase *My little sister said* on the board and read it with children. Note that children can change the words *little sister* to name other people in their families. Have children suggest names of family members they might use (mother, father, uncle, aunt, and so on) and list their suggestions on the board. Then invite children to complete the phrase to write and draw about someone in their own families. Children may wish to dictate to you what it is that this family member says.

Informal Assessment

As children complete the Asking "Me Too" activity note whether they make relevant comments and ask appropriate questions. Also observe whether children try to spell unfamiliar words.

 # Writing

Choices for Writing

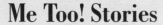

What's the Weather?

Briefly recall the things the big brother liked to do when it was snowy out and the things he liked to do when it was sunny. Then invite children to help you make a weather chart you can keep in the room to record the day's weather.

Greeting Cards

Have children design greeting cards that the little sister might give her brother, or the brother give his little sister. Have children write or dictate messages for inside the cards. If they dictate messages to you, encourage them to help you spell words for which they can supply the initial consonant.

Me Too! Stories

Children may want to make their own *Me Too!* books. Have them brainstorm things they like to do that a friend or relative also likes to do. Record their responses on the board. Children may refer to the list to help them with ideas for their own pages.

Provide each child with two sheets of drawing paper. On the first page, have them draw a thing they like to do and write, or dictate, a sentence about it. On the next page, have them draw a family member who likes to do the same thing. Children should write "Me too!" on this page. Invite children who want to write about more family members to do so.

How Our Families Have Fun

Review some of the ways that the brother and sister have fun together in *Me Too!* Then invite children to dictate a list of ways in which their own families have fun together. Print the list on chart paper. Then read the list with them. Encourage children to illustrate the activities on the chart.

Portfolio Opportunity

Save children's greeting cards as a sample of children's ability to supply the initial consonants in words.

Instruct
and
Integrate

Cross-Curricular Activities

Science

The Four Seasons

Materials
- butcher-block paper
- markers

Invite children to find pages in *Me Too!* that illustrate the seasons summer and winter. Ask if children can name two more seasons. (spring, fall) Discuss how children can tell one season from the other. Talk also about the way people dress and the things they like to do in each season. Then invite children to create a seasonal mural. Divide a large sheet of butcher block paper or a bulletin board in four parts and label the parts *Summer, Winter, Spring,* and *Fall.* Have children work in groups to illustrate a season. Remind them to show in their mural:

- what the weather is like

- how people dress

- what things people like to do

Social Studies

How Families Help One Another

Remind children that the big brother in *Me Too!* shared many things with his little sister and included her in some of the things he liked to do. Point out that he also helped his little sister. Recall ways in which he did this. (helped her ride the skateboard, carried her when she got tired, held her up ice skating, and helped her into the tree house)

Invite children to tell how people in their own families help them. Encourage children to also discuss what they do to help their families. Suggest that children draw and write about their experiences.

Students Acquiring English Encourage children first to discuss with their families how they help and then to report back to the class.

Art

Paper Airplanes

Recall with children that the brother in *Me Too!* had made a paper airplane. Provide children with squares sheets of sturdy drawing paper and show them how to make their own paper airplanes. Encourage children to decorate their airplanes. They can then "fly" their paper airplanes by attaching them to lengths of string and hanging them in the classroom.

Materials
- sturdy drawing paper
- crayons or markers
- tape
- string

Creative

Who Can Balance?

MEETING INDIVIDUAL NEEDS

Challenge Invite children to pantomime the following actions: skateboarding, ice skating, walking across rocks in the water, sledding, and reeling in a fish. Mention to children that they must be able to balance to do each of these activities. Then invite children to see how well they can balance.

- Children can try balancing as they walk across a low-rise balance bar. (Or, they can try balancing as they walk along a piece of thick packing or electrical tape fixed the floor.)

- Children can balance as they step across "construction-stones" in a classroom stream. (NOTE: Be sure to tape down the paper.)

Materials
- low-rise balance bar
- sheets of construction paper
- tape

Theme Assessment Wrap-Up

ASSESSMENT

Reflecting/Self-Assessment

Copy the chart below to distribute to children. Ask them which stories in the theme they liked best. Then discuss what was easy for them and what was more difficult as they read the selections and completed the activities. Have children put a check mark under either *Easy* or *Hard*.

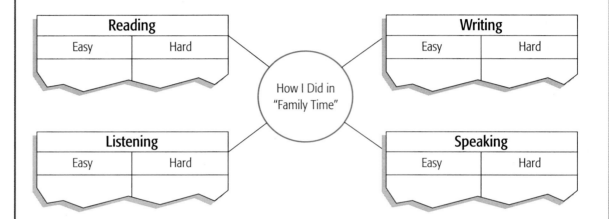

Reading	
Easy	Hard

Writing	
Easy	Hard

How I Did in "Family Time"

Listening	
Easy	Hard

Speaking	
Easy	Hard

Monitoring Literacy Development

There will be many opportunities to observe and evaluate children's literacy development. As children participate in literacy activities, note whether each child has a beginning, a developing, or a proficient understanding of reading, writing, and language concepts. The Observation Checklists, which can be used for recording and evaluating this information, appear in the *Teacher's Assessment Handbook.* They are comprised of the following:

Concepts About Print and Book Handling Behaviors

- Concepts about print
- Book handling

Emergent Reading Behaviors

- Responding to literature
- Storybook rereading
- Decoding strategies

Emergent Writing Behaviors

- Writing
- Stages of Temporary Spelling

Oral Language Behaviors

- Listening attentively
- Listening for information
- Listening to directions
- Listening to books
- Speaking/language development
- Participating in conversations and discussions

Retelling Behaviors

- Retelling a story
- Retelling informational text

Portfolio Opportunity

Invite children to save one piece of work that they did during "Family Time".

Choices for Assessment

Informal Assessment

Review the Observation Checklists and observation notes to determine:

- Did children's responses during and after reading indicate comprehension of the selections?
- How well did children understand the skills presented in this theme? Which skills should be reviewed and practiced in the next theme?
- Did children enjoy the cooperative activities related to the major theme?

Formal Assessment

Select formal tests that meet your classroom needs:

- Kindergarten Literacy Survey
- Theme Skills Test for "Family Time"

See the *Teacher's Assessment Handbook* for guidelines for administering tests and using answer keys and children's sample papers.

Portfolio Assessment

Using Teacher Entry Slips

Teacher entry slips are notes teachers attach to portfolio work. They are particularly useful for noting the purpose of the activity or how well particular students are progressing. Parents appreciate these teacher notes as they review portfolio work.

One easy way to manage teacher entry slips is to create a general slip for the important projects in the portfolio. Describe why students did this activity and what they were learning. Make copies and staple to each student's work.

If you prefer to note specific information about individual students, you can leave a space for additional comments.

Managing Assessment

Using the Theme Assessment Wrap-Up

Question: How can I use the Theme Assessment Wrap-Up?

Answer: Each Theme Assessment Wrap-Up provides a place for children to reflect back on the work they did during the course of a theme. It gives them an opportunity to tell about which selections and activities they found easy or difficult and why. Here are a few tips for using the wrap-up:

- As children explain what they found easy and hard, note their strengths and needs to plan future instruction.

- As an introduction to self-assessment, discuss with children strategies they can use when they find a task difficult.

- Ask children what interested them most. Then discuss with them how during independent reading and writing times they can read other books and do some writing activities that relate to their interests.

For more information on this and other topics, see the *Teacher's Assessment Handbook*.

Celebrating the Theme

Choices for Celebrating

Theme Talk

Invite children to share what they've learned during the theme.

- Talk about the poems they've read or the songs they've sung.

- Review the words (*my, said*) and the beginning sounds (*m, s*). Discuss how knowing these words will help them become readers.

- Invite children to share their favorite writing projects, such as their birthday invitations or cards or their own animal babies and *Me Too!* books. Call on volunteers to read a favorite project to the class.

- Encourage children to name activities that families enjoy doing together and to share some of the things they like to do with their own families. Use the "Our Families" bulletin board to motivate discussion.

See the Houghton Mifflin **Internet** resources for additional theme-related activities.

Self-Assessment

Have children meet in small groups to discuss what they learned in the theme. Use prompts such as the following to foster discussion:

- What interesting things did you learn in the theme?

- How were the families in the theme like your family? How were they different?

Book Talk

Display the theme books. Ask children to tell about the stories and their characters. Encourage children to choose a story and tell how the family members showed they cared about one another.

Materials
- Read Aloud Book: *A Birthday Basket for Tía*
- Big Books: *Animal Mothers; Me Too!*

Our Own Book Fair

Invite children to hold a book fair. Display the books children wrote during the theme around the classroom. Encourage them to explore the books at their leisure. You may also wish to have small groups of children view the books at any one given time. The remaining children, as book authors, can stand by their works and be available for questions or comments.

Materials
- any books written by children

Teacher's Handbook

TABLE OF CONTENTS

Story Retelling Props

Resources
- boat
- retelling figures

Mr. Gumpy's Outing

Children will enjoy using the boat and figures to retell *Mr. Gumpy's Outing.* Invite volunteers to retell the story by taking turns placing the figures one by one into the boat. Encourage children to recall the dialogue between Mr. Gumpy and the other characters. When all the characters are in the boat, children will enjoy tipping them out and retelling the story again.

Materials
- oaktag
- crayons or markers
- scissors
- stapler

Mr. Gumpy's Outing

You can create a boat and crew to help children retell events in *Mr. Gumpy's Outing.* Fold a piece of tagboard and cut it into a 4" x 10" boat shape. Staple the ends of the boat together. Then draw and cut out oaktag forms for a boy, girl, rabbit, cat, dog, pig, sheep, chickens, calf, and goat, and invite children to color them. Have children place the characters in the boat as they retell the story.

INTERACTIVE LEARNING *(continued)*

Ten Black Dots

Children will enjoy recreating the concepts in *Ten Black Dots.* You may want to supply them with sets of black dots, and then give them paper on which they can draw or color. Make the dots by cutting out a 1 1/8" circle from a piece of oaktag to use as a template. Lay the template on top of a sheet of oaktag, and make as many sets of dots as you wish with a black permanent marker. Cut out the dots, make them available to the children, and invite them to use different numbers of dots as parts of pictures they draw. Some children may want to look at the book again to find ideas for their pictures.

Materials
- oaktag
- black marker
- scissors

Ten in a Bed

For *Ten in a Bed,* children will enjoy retelling the story with ten finger puppets. To make finger puppets, cut ten small strips of tagboard short enough to fit around a child's finger. Then tape each strip, end to end, to form ten rings. Cut out ten small tagboard circles and draw a face on each circle. Paste one face onto each ring. Children can take turns wearing all ten rings and removing them one at a time while retelling how the children fell out of bed.

Materials
- oaktag
- scissors
- pencils or markers
- tape

Story Retelling Props

INTERACTIVE LEARNING

Materials

- oaktag
- scissors
- stapler
- crayons or markers

A Birthday Basket for Tia

You can create a basket and props to help children retell events in *A Birthday Basket for Tia*. Fold an 11" x 17" piece of oaktag and cut it into a rounded basket shape. Staple the ends of the basket together. Ask the children to draw, color, and cut out paper versions of the things Cecilia puts in Tia's basket: a book, a bowl, a flowerpot, a tea cup, a red ball, some flowers. As children put objects into the basket, you may want to help them recall why Cecilia chooses these gifts for her aunt.

Materials

- paper plates
- crayons or markers
- craft sticks
- scissors
- glue

Animal Mothers

Have the children work together to make paper plate masks for some or all of the 11 animal mothers featured in the book: cat, lion, baboon, chimpanzee, koala, sloth, kangaroo, elephant, zebra, boar, hedgehog. Help children to cut out the eye holes and glue the plates to craft sticks. Encourage them to help each other remember how each mother carries or travels with her baby. Children can take turns holding up the masks and speaking as if they were the mother animals telling how they carry or travel with their babies.

INTERACTIVE LEARNING *(continued)*

Me Too!

To prepare for the retelling, stand up the prop board and make the stick-on pieces available to the children. Invite pairs of children to take turns playing the brother and the little sister. Encourage the child who is playing the brother to select a stick-on piece, place it in the appropriate spot on the prop board, and role-play the scene in which it appears in the story. Have the child who is playing the sister respond with "Me too." When they reach the candy cane piece, the sister should say, "You too," and place the stick-on piece in the appropriate space on the prop board.

Resources
• stick-on retelling pieces
• prop board

Me Too!

Children will enjoy using oaktag and two empty shoeboxes to act out scenes from *Me Too!* Label one shoebox "Me too," and the other "You too." Then draw or cut from oaktag the following shapes: skateboard, airplane, backpack, football, tree house, sled, ice skates, cake, fishing pole, and candy cane. Encourage children to help color or decorate the shapes. Make the objects available to children. They can then place each item in the appropriate box and retell the story in a similar fashion to that described above.

Materials
• shoe boxes
• oaktag
• crayons or markers
• scissors

Games

Resources

- Monkey Business game board
- Tokens

Monkey Business

Players: Two–Four

Preparation Have each child choose a different color token and place it on the space labeled START.

Directions In turn, each player:

1. Spins to a small letter and names it.

2. Moves his or her marker to the next space on the board that has the matching capital letter.

3. Continues playing until one player reaches FINISH. If a player spins to a letter that is not ahead of his or her token, the player moves directly to FINISH and wins.

Animal Puzzles

Players: One or More

Here is an additional game idea to reinforce identification of capital and small letters.

Preparation Draw an animal on a large square sheet of construction paper . Cut the sheet in two pieces to create a puzzle. Print capital Q on the upper half of the animal and small q on the bottom half. Create additional puzzles using the letters: *R-r, L-l, N-n, B-b, E-e, G-g,* and *F-f.* Cut the puzzles in a variety of animal shapes.

Directions Players work individually or in pairs to complete the puzzles by matching capital and small letters to form animals.

Materials
- Large sheets of construction paper

Games

Busy Families

Players: Two

Resources
- Busy Families game board
- Tokens

Preparation Have each child choose a group of tokens of one color. Name each picture on the game board with children: *soap, soccer ball, milk, soup, socks, mat, map, mop, music, saw.* Name both letters on the spinner: *m* and *s*.

Directions In turn, each player:

1. Spins the spinner.

2. Names the letter it points to.

3. Finds and names an object in the boxes at the center of the game board that begins with the sound of the indicated letter and places a token on that object.

4. Play continues until all the objects are covered. The player with the most tokens on the board wins.

INTERACTIVE LEARNING *(continued)*

Additional Game Idea: Letter Toss

Players: Two–Four

Here is an additional game idea to reinforce listening for beginning sounds.

Preparation Divide a large sheet of butcher paper into eight squares. In each square, draw one of the following pictures: *mouse, saw, moon, sock, salt, mask, sun, milk.* Tape the paper to the floor. Name the pictures with children.

Directions In turn, each player:

1. Tosses the two beanbags, one at a time, aiming for a picture whose name begins with the sound of the letter on the beanbag. For each successful toss, the player gets one point.

2. Each player gets three turns. The player with more points wins.

Materials
- Two beanbags: one marked with the letter *s*, the other with the letter *m*
- Large sheet of butcher paper

John Jacob Jingleheimer Schmidt

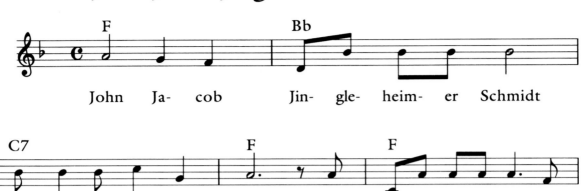

John   Ja-   cob   Jin-   gle-   heim-   er   Schmidt

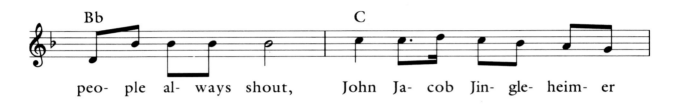

His   name   is   my   name   too.   When   ev-   er   we   go   out   The

peo-   ple   al-   ways   shout,   John   Ja-   cob   Jin-   gle-   heim-   er

Schmidt.   Dah   Dah   Dah   Dah,   Dah   Dah   Dah.

Row, Row, Row Your Boat

Row, row, row your boat gent- ly down the

stream; ___ Mer- ri- ly, mer- ri- ly, mer- ri- ly, mer- ri- ly,

Life is but a dream. ___

Our Family

LINDA ARNOLD

Me and my mo- ther   Me and my broth- er

Me and my Dad __ dy   Me and my Mom __

Sing- ing a song __ __ a- bout our fam- i- ly

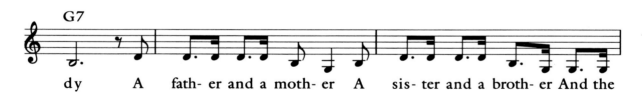

Me and my moth- er   Me and my broth- er   Me and my Dad -

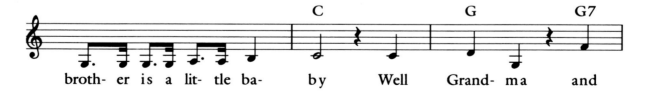

dy   A fath- er and a moth- er A sis- ter and a broth- er And the

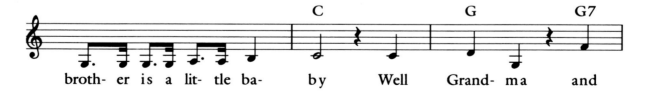

broth- er is a lit- tle ba- by   Well   Grand- ma and

Our Family (continued)

Grand- pa   are   part of the fam- i-

ly And Grand- ma and Grand- pa   sure love

me   Me and my mo- ther   Me and my broth- er

Me and my Dad __   dy   Me and my Mom __

sing- ing a song __ __ a- bout our fam- i-   ly

Others Are Special

LOIS RAEBECK

Oh,   I'm ver- y spec- ial as   you can see, but

man- y oth- er peo- ple are   spec- ial like me!   There's

moth- er and fath- er, and   sis- ter and bro- ther and   unc- le and aunt _ and

grand- ma and grand- pa and   friends at school!   Friends at school!

All   are   spec- ial   like   me   and   you!

Audio-Visual Resources

Adventure Productions
3404 Terry Lake Road
Ft. Collins, CO 80524

AIMS Media
9710 DeSoto Avenue
Chatsworth, CA
91311-4409
800-367-2467

Alfred Higgins Productions
6350 Laurel Canyon
Blvd.
N. Hollywood, CA
91606
800-766-5353

**American School
Publishers/SRA**
P.O. Box 543
Blacklick, OH
43004-0543
800-843-8855

Audio Bookshelf
R.R. #1, Box 706
Belfast, ME 04915
800-234-1713

Audio Editions
Box 6930
Auburn, CA 95604-6930
800-231-4261

Audio Partners, Inc.
Box 6930
Auburn, CA 95604-6930
800-231-4261

Bantam Doubleday Dell
1540 Broadway
New York, NY 10036
212-782-9652

Barr Films
12801 Schabarum Ave.
Irwindale, CA 97106
800-234-7878

Bullfrog Films
Box 149
Oley, PA 19547
800-543-3764

Churchill Films
12210 Nebraska Ave.
Los Angeles, CA 90025
800-334-7830

Clearvue/EAV
6465 Avondale Ave.
Chicago, IL 60631
800-253-2788

Coronet/MTI
108 Wilmot Road
Deerfield, IL 60015
800-777-8100

Creative Video Concepts
5758 SW Calusa Loop
Tualatin, OR 97062

**Dial Books for Young
Readers**
375 Hudson St.
New York, NY 10014
800-526-0275

Direct Cinema Ltd.
P.O. Box 10003
Santa Monica, CA 90410
800-525-0000

**Disney Educational
Production**
105 Terry Drive,
Suite 120
Newtown, PA 18940
800-295-5010

Encounter Video
2550 NW Usshur
Portland, OR 97210
800-677-7607

Filmic Archives
The Cinema Center
Botsford, CT 06404
800-366-1920

**Films for Humanities and
Science**
P.O. Box 2053
Princeton, NJ 08543
609-275-1400

Finley-Holiday
12607 E. Philadelphia St.
Whittier, CA 90601

Fulcrum Publishing
350 Indiana St.
Golden, CO 80401

G.K. Hall
Box 500, 100 Front St.
Riverside, NJ 08057

HarperAudio
10 East 53rd Street
New York, NY 10022
212-207-6901

Hi-Tops Video
2730 Wiltshire Blvd.
Suite 500
Santa Monica, CA 90403
213-216-7900

Houghton Mifflin/Clarion
Wayside Road
Burlington, MA 01803
800-225-3362

Idaho Public TV/Echo Films
1455 North Orchard
Boise, ID 83706
800-424-7963

Kidvidz
618 Centre St.
Newton, MA 02158
617-965-3345

L.D.M.I.
P.O. Box 1445,
St. Laurent
Quebec, Canada H4L
4Z1

Let's Create
50 Cherry Hill Rd.
Parsippany, NJ 07054

Listening Library
One Park Avenue
Old Greenwich, CT
06870
800-243-4504

Live Oak Media
P.O. Box 652
Pine Plains, NY 12567
518-398-1010

Mazon Productions
3821 Medford Circle
Northbrook, IL 60062
708-272-2824

Media Basics
Lighthouse Square
705 Boston Post Road
Guildford, CT 06437
800-542-2505

MGM/UA Home Video
1000 W. Washington
Blvd.
Culver City, CA 90232
310-280-6000

Milestone Film and Video
275 W. 96th St.,
Suite 28C
New York, NY 10025

Miramar
200 Second Ave.
Seattle, WA 98119
800-245-6472

Audio-Visual Resources (continued)

National Geographic
Educational Services
Washington, DC 20036
800-548-9797

The Nature Company
P.O. Box 188
Florence, KY 41022
800-227-1114

Philomel
1 Grosset Drive
Kirkwood, NY 13795
800-847-5575

Premiere Home Video
755 N. Highland
Hollywood, CA 90038
213-934-8903

Puffin Books
375 Hudson St.
New York, NY 10014

Rabbit Ears
131 Rowayton Avenue
Rowayton, CT 06853
800-800-3277

Rainbow Educational Media
170 Keyland Court
Bohemia, NY 11716
800-331-4047

Random House Media
400 Hahn Road
Westminster, MD 21157
800-733-3000

Reading Adventure
7030 Huntley Road,
Unit B
Columbus, OH 43229

Recorded Books
270 Skipjack Road
Prince Frederick,
MD 20678
800-638-1304

SelectVideo
7200 E. Dry Creek Rd.
Englewood, CO 80112
800-742-1455

Silo/Alcazar
Box 429, Dept. 318
Waterbury, VT 05676

Spoken Arts
10100 SBF Drive
Pinellas Park, FL 34666
800-126-8090

SRA
P.O. Box 543
Blacklick, OH
43004-0543
800-843-8855

Strand/VCI
3350 Ocean Park Blvd.
Santa Monica, CA 90405
800-922-3827

Taliesin Productions
558 Grove St.
Newton, MA 02162
617-332-7397

Time-Life Education
P.O. Box 85026
Richmond, VA
23285-5026
800-449-2010

Video Project
5332 College Ave.
Oakland, CA 94618
800-475-2638

Warner Home Video
4000 Warner Blvd.
Burbank, CA 91522
818-243-5020

Weston Woods
Weston, CT 06883
800-243-5020

Wilderness Video
P.O. Box 2175
Redondo Beach, CA
90278
310-539-8573

BOOKS AVAILABLE IN SPANISH
Spanish editions of English titles referred to in the Bibliography are available from the following publishers or distributors.

Bilingual Educational Services, Inc.
2514 South Grand Ave.
Los Angeles, CA
90007-9979
800-448-6032

Charlesbridge
85 Main Street
Watertown, MA 02172
617-926-5720

Children's Book Press
6400 Hollis St., Suite 4
Emeryville, CA 94608
510-655-3395

Childrens Press
5440 N. Cumberland Ave.
Chicago, IL 60656-1469
800-621-1115

Econo-Clad Books
P.O. Box 1777
Topeka, KS 66601
800-628-2410

Farrar, Straus, & Giroux
9 Union Square
New York, NY 10003
212-741-6973

Harcourt Brace
6277 Sea Harbor Drive
Orlando, FL 32887
800-225-5425

HarperCollins
10 E. 53rd Street
New York, NY 10022
717-941-1500

Holiday House
425 Madison Ave.
New York, NY 10017
212-688-0085

Kane/Miller
Box 310529
Brooklyn, NY
11231-0529
718-624-5120

Alfred A. Knopf
201 E. 50th St.
New York, NY 10022
800-638-6460

Lectorum
111 Eighth Ave.
New York, NY 10011
800-345-5946

Santillana
901 W. Walnut St.
Compton, CA 90220
800-245-8584

Simon and Schuster
866 Third Avenue
New York, NY 10022
800-223-2336

Viking
357 Hudson Street
New York, NY 10014
212-366-2000

Index

graphic sources
    calendars, reading, T45
    graph, T57
reference sources
    dictionary, T146, T173
    magazines, using, T31
    maps, using, T113, T124, T152
    newspapers, using, T36
    reference books, T144, T152
study strategies
    directions, following, T57, T59,
        T75, T85, T124, T125

Study strategies. *See* Skills, major; Strategies, reading; Study skills.

Summarizing
    oral summaries, T20, T70, T76,
        T112, T116, T118, T136, T140

T

Teacher-guided reading. *See* Reading modes.

Teaching across the curriculum. *See* Content areas, reading in the; Cross-curricular activities.

Teaching and management
    grouping students flexibly, T10,
        T102, T127, T155
    managing assessment, T10, T102
    managing instruction, T10, T102,
        T127, T155
    special needs of students, meeting.
        See Individual needs, meeting.
    teaching tips, T87, T179

Technology resources
    Internet, Houghton Mifflin, T7,
        T12, T15, T35, T65, T94, T99,
        T104, T107, T127, T155, T186

Text organization, T135, T144

Theme, celebrating, T94, T186

Theme concepts, T9, T12, T94, T104, T186

Theme, launching the, T12, T104

Theme projects, T12, T94, T104, T186

Theme
    Family Time, T95–T186
    Just for Fun, T3–T94

Think About Words
    picture clues, **T40, T78, T138, T166**
    sounds for letters, T138, T166
    what makes sense, **T40, T78, T138, T166**

Think Aloud, T18, T21, T23, T25, T41,

T43, T45, T47, T53, T69, T73, T75,
T79, T110, T111, T113, T116,
T129, T133, T163

Thinking
    creatively. *See* Creative thinking.
    critically. *See* Critical thinking.

U

Usage. *See* Language and usage.

V

Videotapes, T99, T149

Viewing
    environment, T28, T55, T57, T63,
        T150
    illustrations, T12, T16, T25, T39,
        T44, T47, T57, T66, T68, T69,
        T71, T73, T79, T78, T80, T86,
        T110, T111, T114, T118, T128,
        T134, T135, T136, T138,
        T139, T143, T144, T145, T150,
        T157, T159
    photographs, T12, T104, T144,
        T150
    purpose
        to analyze, T63, T66, T76, T77
        to compare/contrast, T44,
            T104, T114, T131, T138,
            T139, T143
        to observe patterns, T45
        to make observations, T12,
            T16, T25, T39, T44, T47,
            T57, T66, T68, T69, T71,
            T73, T79, T78, T80, T86,
            T110, T111, T114, T118,
            T128, T134, T135, T136,
            T138, T139, T143, T144,
            T145, T150, T157, T159
    television/movies, T131
    text, T51, T70, T73, T84, T128,
        T142, T174

Visual literacy. *See* Cross-curricular activities.

Visualizing, T31, T61

Vocabulary, extending
    action words, T30
    alliteration, T118, **T121**
    animal names, **T21**
    animal words, T148
    color words, T57, T61
    expansion, T148

family words, T122
games, T30, T59, T60, T84, T149,
    T175
naming words, T30
opposites, T111
parts of body, T21
rhyme, T23, T25, T54, T59, T85,
    T115, T166
Spanish words, T108, T109, T110,
    T112, T113, T114, T115, T122
synonyms, T111
unfamiliar word meaning, T19,
    T21, T41, T112, T113, T131,
    T132, T136, T138, T148, T160
using context, T40, T78, T138,
    T160, T166
using word webs, T129, T157
visual clues, T40, T49, T76, T138,
    T160, T166
word meaning, T19, T20, T21,
    T22, T30, T41, T47, T112,
    T113, T114, T115, T131, T132,
    T136, T138, T148, T159, T160
word wall, T151

W

Watch Me Read books
    Snowfun by Penny Carter,
        T178
    Surprise! by Susan
        Meddaugh, T86

Word analysis. *See* Think About Words; Vocabulary, extending.

Word webs, T30, T61, T88, T129, T157

Writer's log. *See* Journal.

Writer's craft
    alliteration, **T111,** T118, **T121**
    language patterns, T142, T150,
        T170, T178
    repetition, T17, T70, T71, T72, T85

Writing
    choices
        animal book, T61, T151
        birthday card, T123
        book, T89
        card, T181
        description, T61, T89
        invitation, T123
        list, T151, T181
        menu, T31
        message, T123